FROM

BADASS LEADER

FROM **BAD** TO
BADASS LEADER

12 LEADERSHIP LESSONS

LIVE TO LEAD

MICHELLE D. REINES

MDR COACHING & CONSULTING, INC.

Let's stay connected, visit our website for various tools and book updates, go to: https://badassleader.com/gift

Printed in the United States of America

"Truly unlike any other leadership book I've read in the past. Michelle's story is inspiring and motivational; I really appreciated how she had the guts to share all of her mistakes and hard knocks before turning them into important life lessons. The book is just as entertaining as it is educational, and will appeal not only to established industry leaders, but to the next up-and-coming generation. As a passionate filmmaker and motorcyclist, stories of grit and determination always appeal to me. A great ride, and a great read."

#EnjoytheRead #LivetoLead #WhyWeRide #MOTOvational

— *Bryan H. Carroll*
Director, WHY WE RIDE

CONTENTS

FOREWORD

When Michelle reached out to me and asked me to review her book and consider writing her Foreword, I wondered why me? After meeting her and hearing what she hoped to accomplish by sharing her story, I understood. She shared she chose to invite me to write her foreword because she was moved and inspired by our story, the casualness of our brand and what we value as leaders and as a family. After reading through her lessons and what she refers to as her bumps and bruises along the way, I knew I wanted to be a part of supporting her goal in preventing others from enduring what she calls "bull rides." Her book, *From Bad to Badass Leader,* is a book of her lessons learned—the good, bad and some not so cool stuff, too. I especially enjoyed that this book is different than many other leadership books. It really is like you literally sat down with her and had a casual conversation about what she's experienced, learned, how she's struggled, been humbled and her foot-in-mouth moments. Yes, she shares some victories and triumphs too—but it's quite vulnerable. She doesn't hesitate to tell on herself; she wants her readers to know that leadership is not perfect—it's an evolution. She hopes her stories will help her readers avoid some of the same pitfalls and hopefully save them and their teams from some of the growing pains of learning how to lead themselves and others.

Michelle also put a lot of effort into sharing strategies, words of caution and advice based on her journey or what she calls her ride. There's a thoughtful flow to the lessons; it makes sense why they are served up in the order she's framed them 1 through 12. I really enjoyed the informality and playfulness of her writing style, too. It kept me engaged and entertained, and I really did learn the lessons by the end. I found value in reading through and not skipping over the stories and was intrigued with how surprisingly well her outside-the-box creativity worked when it came to her use of hashtags and rehashing versus a more formal lesson summary. I thought that was a great way to have readers experience the lessons and not rush to a summary. She believes stories make lessons stickier. I'd have to agree, and oddly enough for someone from my generation, so did the hashtags.

When I originally met with Michelle, she shared she really wanted to create a brand that was approachable, playful, appealed to and intrigued leaders who might not otherwise want to read a more corporate style leadership book. She wanted to write the book that she felt she needed back when she was "on the bull." As I stated in my February 2019 Orange County Weekly interview, "I want people to know that it's okay to think differently"—"To do things that haven't been done." With her book and bold unconventional Badass Leader brand, I believe she's done that. I trust you will—in her words—"enjoy the ride" and hopefully think about your own while learning from and being entertained by hers. Enjoy!

ALOHA ~ WING

Wing Lam is the Founder/Co-owner of Wahoo's Fish Taco. Wahoo's just celebrated its 30th anniversary, with more than 60 locations across the U.S. and Japan.

LETTER TO ASPIRING BADASS LEADERS

What this book is <u>not</u>, is a leadership academic resource, filled with principles, methodologies, laws or processes—it's a conversation. It's like we sat down and shared stories over an ice-cold beer or chilled tequila on a hot, sunny day.

It is an unconventional leadership book, an autobiography of lessons learned. By reading this book, you'll be taken on a ride with me through my personal leadership story, I call my journey or ride. While you're reading the tales of my woes and cat-howl moments, I encourage you to think about your own ride, your stories and how my experiences might offer you some insight into what's happening on your journey.

Although our specific trades or crafts might be different, don't be too quick to skip over the details of the ride. The lessons are in the stories. Stories make lessons stickier, like lock-tight to a nut & bolt. Challenge yourself to find the similarities that might be happening in your life. Fix what's not working or no longer fits and cat-howl, growl and pound your chest for the stuff you've got dialed-in. Then get out there and pay it forward. Help develop other badass leaders by sharing your lessons learned. Yes, the good, bad and ugly!

If you haven't already, I'd love it if you'd Join the Club on our website, so we can keep this thing going and support one another. We're just getting started. #ExpandYourTribe

Spread the word, share the book, wear the t-shirt, help us support other badass leaders.

#NOBULLRIDES

Thank you so much for reading my story. I look forward to hearing yours and hope I have somehow helped you. This is my first book, so I'm a rookie at this stuff—I really hope you enjoy it, and please share it.

With love and gratitude,

Michelle

#Ciao4Now #NotYourMothersLeadershipBook

THE DEALEO

Look, this book isn't for everyone. Some people will not enjoy my style of communication, and that's okay; there's another book out there for you. I'm not an English major, doctor, or psychologist. I am an operational leader, much like many of you. This book appeals to leaders with an edge, like me, who ask for forgiveness more often than permission. Perhaps you're an up-and-coming leader, entrepreneur, or executive—who's received a few bruises of your own and want to take your badass leader competencies to the next level. If so, pull up a chair, grab a sip of good tequila (#Casamigos™ is one of my favs), and come along for the ride. This is my story. I'm sharing it with the hope that somebody out there will benefit from the epic failures, wins, and lessons I've learned throughout my imperfect and awesome leadership ride.

So, here's the dealeo. By reading this book, you'll realize these stories and lessons are transferable into any industry. It doesn't matter who you work for; people are people and business is business. Enjoy my story and apply it to your own. Most Badass Leaders will be eager to evaluate themselves to see if the boots fit. For some, that might involve "embracing the suck," as David Goggins, author, retired Navy Seal and probably the toughest man alive so unapologetically puts it. "Embracing the suck" is military slang, loosely defined as consciously accepting something that might be challenging or even unpleasant. I have had to embrace the suck during some of the most stressful moments in my career, entrepreneurship, and personal life. Let's be candid. Sometimes moments in life suck, challenges suck, or we suck as leaders, and even as spouses, partners or parents. I sure know I have at times. The road to becoming a Badass Leader will include trials and errors, successes and failures—boot-in-mouth moments. It is not an easy ride. It's messy and sometimes painful. Growth can be uncomfortable. We need to have failures and missteps, or we aren't pushing the limits of our own potential. I love how Tony Robbins, author, life coach, and philanthropist, refers to the Six Human Needs, "If you're not growing, you're dying." I wholeheartedly believe that. Yes, I'm a Robbins fan. This book is an invitation for you to grow—to take yourself, your team and your organization to the next level by awakening the Badass Leader within.

BADASS LEADER DEFINED

It's not a title—it's a way of being. **Being a Badass Leader is about fearlessness and challenging yourself and others to go after what's possible.** Being badass, however, is not about being reckless; it's about stretching yourself. As Tony Robbins might encourage you as a leader of people—walk over the fire! A Badass Leader is someone who strives to thrive outside their comfort zone. They are responsibly fearless and vulnerable. They focus on people over performance and rock their talk—someone who embodies many of the behaviors embedded in the 12 Leadership Lessons that follow. #BadassLeader

Being badass goes beyond the boardroom. It includes how we show up in life. Badass Leaders don't participate in or tolerate bully-like behaviors, in real life or on social media. I am not just talking about hard-ass bullying, I am talking about snide comments. They aren't necessary, don't add value, and hurt others. That's not cool, and it's certainly not Badass Leader behavior. Being a Badass Leader means you care about people, animals, our communities, organizations, and our planet. A badass is someone who endeavors to do the right thing and remains ravenous for knowledge and eager to help others. A badass is someone who's qualitatively successful. This is who I strive to be and how I define badass. More importantly, how do you define it for yourself? That's what really matters.

Keep in mind, during your leadership ride, there may be times when you're uncertain, especially when taking risks or living outside of your comfort zone. That's ok, strap on your helmet and some badass wings, and go for it! #LivetoLead

INTRODUCTION/RIDE

Throughout my continuing leadership evolution, I have discovered what works for me as a leader of teams. I don't even consider myself to be an author really, until now. I am a leader, possibly much like you. In the stories that follow, I share tips, behaviors, strategies, and the lessons I've learned that have supported me in pushing myself and teams to unearth our inner badasses.

These behaviors didn't come naturally, and some of them didn't come easily at first. It is important to note that when I share what worked, I am not referring to myself as a leader without flaws, trials, tribulations, or failures. Nor am I asserting that I consider myself to be better than anyone else. These behaviors were born throughout my leadership ride, with the guidance and tough feedback from various badass mentors, life experiences, kick-ass results, and absolutely embracing the suck when things got tough along the way—all in pursuit of fulfilling my desire to become a Badass Leader. I believe, deep inside we all want to be Badass Leaders.

MEET MICHELLE

Michelle is a speaker, author, entrepreneur, CEO, and an ever-evolving Badass Leader. Her definition of "Badass Leader" is being intentional about who she wants and needs to be for her team. Early in her leadership journey she was an absolute ass as a boss, oblivious to the impact she was having on people. Perhaps, much like many of you, she didn't understand the art of leading people, communicating and building a Badass Team. The people part can be the most challenging for many leaders. It certainly was for her. She's excited to share the most impactful 12 Leadership Lessons she's learned during her over 30-year corporate career. These stories and lessons are focused on the people part of leadership. Follow these 12 lessons and you unlock the art of leading like a Badass.

Michelle is a Strategic Interventionist, certified by the man of transformation himself, Tony Robbins, and his partner Cloe Madanes. Today, not only is Michelle an author and creator of the Badass Leader brand, she is the founder of MDR Coaching & Consulting, Inc., a leadership development company. In addition to working with amazing leaders and teams, she is an authorized partner for multiple Wiley Brand resources, and is proud to be a member of the Channel Partner Network for the Ken Blanchard Companies. Michelle looks forward to sharing her thrills of victory, as well as some agonies of defeat, with a goal of supporting you as you embrace the success and the suck throughout your Badass Leadership ride. She is manically committed to continuous improvement, and to, quite frankly, being badass . . . as a leader, a woman, a wife and an entrepreneur.

#ThrillsandAgony

INSPIRATION

So, what was my inspiration for this book? The inspiration for writing this book and starting these brands were born out of what I now refer to as my #BullRide. My bull ride was the consequence of my cataclysmic leadership failure, resulting in a HUGE serving of humble pie. I very quickly learned to appreciate the profound impact an unconscious leader has on people, teams, and organizational health and performance. The significance and value of a team became abundantly clear, as did the critical importance and necessity for me to immediately begin evolving as a leader. This painfully humbling experience (the suck) set the course correction for what would become a lifelong hunger for leadership growth and contribution—a self-prescribed reparation in many ways, shared through my 12 Leadership Lessons.

#HumblePie

LOGO DESIGN

Wings—Wings represent growth, risk, and possibility to support you in striving to live outside of your comfort zone, and because they're badass.

Helmet—The helmet is a reminder to use your smarts. Protect yourself from a bull ride, and safely navigate yourself and your teams through the struggle.

12—My 12 Leadership Lessons from my journey/ride, of course.

Motorcycle Theme—I met my hubby at a biker bar: Cook's Corner in Southern California. We love adventure! Motorcycles are a huge part of our life—work hard, play harder is our motto!
#ThisBrands4U

#CooksCorner

EXPECTATIONS

This is not your mother's leadership book. It's a book of shared lessons and boot-in-mouth moments. I wrote this for you. I'm a kinesthetic learner, which means I learn best through connecting with stories (the feeling I get when connecting through shared experiences). You will see, hear and feel my stories and hopefully learn, grow, laugh and be moved too. Connect these stories to yours. Let's continue this ride together.

This book is crafted like a leadership layer cake. Each layer builds on the previous one, so by the time you arrive at Lesson 12, you've hopefully got it! I have purposefully echoed and stacked the lessons and built upon the stories to support you in walking away with a clear understanding of what worked for me, so you can craft a badass roadmap that will work for you. In coaching and neurolinguistics (fancy talk), we call that unconscious competence. It's like sleep walking, but you know where you're going. Lol. Clear as mud, right? That means you get it; you can recite it forwards and backwards because it stacks. Stacks like layers of yummy cake with an ice-cold milk chaser. #LikeLayerCake #Stacks #12Lessons. Oh, and yes, lots of #Hashtags and #Rehashing going on. Hope it clicks as you continue the ride. #OutsideBoxes #TakingRisks #BeingDifferent #NotSameSame #LessonsInStories

#HASHTAGS & #REHASHES

What's up with the #Hashtags?

Work can be so serious sometimes, so can leadership and vulnerability. I'm a fan of being casual, playful and connected. In my first-time rookie writing experience, #Hashtags kinda did that for me. Maybe it is because there were so many bumps and bruises shared, it made me more comfortable. I will leave that psychoanalysis to the true experts. Lol. Plus, I personally love #Nicknames!

I have candidly disclosed that this book isn't for everyone. Fortunately for some, there are plenty of exceptional books that follow the status quo; this isn't one of them. Bottom line, I am sharing myself with all of you, no pretense, not perfect—just me. #Hashtags and all.

#Rehashing vs. Summaries

Why did I choose to use #Rehashes in place of traditional style Lesson/ Chapter summaries?

1. First off, if you're reading this book, I have a belief that you're comfortable with risk, being different, thinking outside of the box, and enjoy being playful. So, I figured my readers are open to taking the trail less or never traveled. As such, I feel comfortable doing summaries differently with and for you. Maybe it will be proven to have been a #Bust or a #BombDiggity. I am hoping for the latter. #WinkWink ☺

2. I am inviting you to metaphorically hop on the back and come along for the ride. Immerse yourself in the stories. Kick back, enjoy a hot or cold one. Don't rush it; take in the scenery as they say. Remember,

stories make lessons stickier, like lock-tight to a nut & bolt. The #Rehashes at the end of each lesson won't make sense if you don't. I was purposeful in using #Rehashes in hope of discouraging you from jumping ahead to a summary and missing out on the journey. The lessons are embedded in the stories. If a book summary is your preference, I would invite you to explore where else in your life you are perhaps missing out on the journey, because you are rushing to a destination? I hope you'll choose to make your journey through this book fun and enjoyable. #Cheers

3. I also wanted to create an experience for you, like a word or #Hashtag puzzle to micro-summarize each lesson in a unique yet memorable way. I have even test driven the #Rehashing with a few early readers prior to editorial reviews. The feedback was pretty cool and exciting on how well they worked. I hope they'll do the same for you. It's like #SpeedHashing #GoWithTheFlow #EnjoyTheRide #NotSameSame #Different

DEDICATION

I dedicate this book to the Badass Teams, leaders, and mentors whom I've had the privilege of working with and for, throughout my career. I didn't do this alone, the credit is theirs, they created the space or the struggle for me to grow. Our time together continues to live in my heart, my mind, and through our collective accomplishments and memories. I am so appreciative and proud of you all. I miss and cherish each of you and celebrate your growth, transformation through the suck, and cat-howling to your successes both personally and professionally. To my teams, thank you all for trusting me and allowing me to push/pull hard, while creating the struggle. Thanks for stepping up and playing your asses off, continually evolving as a team, rising to each and every challenge, always committed to making it happen. This book is dedicated to YOU, and what I have learned from you during my ride. Being a Badass Leader is not a destination, it's an evolution. Keep on keepin' on!

—*Coach Reines*

LESSON 1:
DON'T BE AN ASS!

LESSON 1
DON'T BE AN ASS!

#BullRide

To put it politely, I was an ass. To make things worse, I was oblivious to that fact. I'm sure the same is true for many leaders. My wakeup calls, fortunately for me, happened when I was a very young, up-and-coming leader—manager really. I didn't have any leadership competency to speak of at that point in my career. I refer to this experience in my life as my bull ride. It occurred in the early 1990s when I was an unapologetic, self-important 26-year-old . . . fill-in-the blank with whatever unbecoming word that comes to mind.

I was working in the Atlanta marketplace for an amazing company. Like many people who get promoted to their level of incompetence, I was hard-working, competitive, dominant, and extremely results-oriented. I set outrageous goals and worked my ass off to achieve them. I was extremely passionate about my work and would even describe myself as someone who was obsessed with work and addicted to achieving results—not in a healthy way either.

When I first started, there was a top-performing associate by the name of Crystal. She held the record for the greatest volume of leases ever—an undefeated champion! Very shortly after I was hired, I brazenly set out to double her record. I definitely played win-lose back then. When I achieved that insane goal, it earned the attention of the powers that be and put me on the fast track for growth and opportunity. My first mini-leadership role was a very short stint with a team of three—a small step-up to a 150-unit lease-up property in Gainesville, Georgia for approximately six months, resulting in yet another promotion—this one much bigger.

I was offered a dream opportunity to relocate to downtown Chicago as a general manager for a 25-story luxury residential high-rise, with an in-place team of 18 people—big step up indeed. I was stoked and very proud of myself. I'd done it! I was 26 years old living on the top floor of a downtown Chicago skyscraper with a badass apartment and a generous salary for my age, an opportunity of a lifetime for sure. I was hyper-focused on being the best manager they ever had.

It was a fast move. I flew to Chicago, interviewed on Friday afternoon, returned home that evening, packed suitcases, and flew back Sunday to my new life as a Chicagoan. I was walking on sunshine. In a moment's notice, I left close friends, my family, and boyfriend, Mike. I left my car behind for a friend to sell, then hopped on a plane and never looked back.

Off I went, alone, to begin a new chapter of my life in a massive, incredible city. To say I didn't know what I didn't know, is an outrageous understatement. In the 1990s, the Chicago market was pretty much a guy's-game. Imagine a 26-year-old female with a southern accent, responsible for approximately a $90 million business. I came out of the gate hell bent on making my mark and proving myself to my father, my company, and to my new team. I wanted to show them just how awesome I was. At this immature age, it was all about proving myself, taking credit, and asserting my power. After all, I was the boss. #RuhRoh

The interesting thing, and what I see happen often in my current role, is that when dominant personality types push their teams really hard for performance, it absolutely can (and in my case, did) move results upward. It's what I call the illusion of success. It's not sustainable, nor is it healthy. This illusion of success can put leaders into a risky predicament. They might actually believe what they're doing is sustainable. However, in the long run, it actually does the opposite. It's destructive and leads to declining performance over time, eroding trust, and compromising the potential of people and organizations along the way.

At some point, there will be collateral damage, and for me it came in the form of resignations. There was a walk-out, along with some very colorful and candid feedback about what a "B" I was, sprinkled with a load of other very accurate, well-deserved colorful adjectives. The most appalling part of this whole leadership disaster was the fact that I was completely lacking the self-awareness of what an absolute ass I was as a boss. I never saw it coming.

Unbelievable! My initial reaction that morning was, "How dare they conspire behind my back to resign! What is wrong with these people?" There was no denying only one common denominator existed, and it was me. I was the problem, and I was going to have to face the consequences, which at that time could potentially have included being fired, losing my fabulous downtown Chicago apartment, and having to head back to Atlanta, an epic failure—a bitter pill indeed for my massive ego. I was dumbfounded, distraught, infuriated, scared, and at this early stage in the game, I didn't have two nickels to rub together, or even a car to drive back home.

Even worse, I had to call the man who had given me this incredible opportunity, to let him know what happened. Keep in mind, the company had to have invested around $10,000 to relocate me. I remember calling him and thinking to myself, how do I even start this conversation? "Hi, I hope you had a nice weekend. I'm calling to let you know UMMMMMMM, my team just walked out on me and told me I was a raging bitch." Not their words. Mine.

I don't remember the exact words that came out of my mouth. I just remember my heartbeat pounding in my ears, my voice shaking uncontrollably, and having difficulty breathing. I was rightfully panicked! My boss came to see me, and it took him about an hour with traffic to get to me. Thank God. I needed that time to gather myself, settle my emotions, and think about what just happened. I was still reeling, but also realized that this was completely my fault. There was no denying that I created this epic failure, and it was time to face the consequences, or what I now refer to as: step up and embrace the suck.

#Suckit

It was entirely possible that in seven days' time I would be not only unemployed, but possibly homeless, without anything but debt and shame. My ego and pride were still pretty massive in spite of getting beat up by this experience. I wasn't about to call family or friends for any help. I was going to dig myself out of this self-created sh*t show one way or another—alone. This was going to require owning up to the mess I created. So, when he arrived, he sat with me in my office for a few minutes. As I desperately struggled to compose myself, he looked me in the eye while listening to my account of what transpired. He then asked me one of the most difficult questions I've ever been asked before, "What would you do if you were me?"

I hated and respected him for asking me that question. It was time to embrace the suck. #EmbracetheSuck. Through tear-filled eyes, I held his gaze and said, "I'd fire me." Saying those words out loud killed me. I hated admitting, if our roles were reversed, I would've absolutely fired him.

He paused for a moment, then said something along the lines of "Well I'm not going to do that." I looked at him, feeling very confused and started to bawl openly—a very ugly cry.

My boss was a leader, who didn't show very much emotion for good or bad, he then calmly explained why he was not firing me. He said that he was also partly responsible for my failure. He went on to say things like he should've supported me more. I needed development and leadership training, but he saw potential in me. I was still in a daze. I do recall him sharing that he wouldn't be the one training me and I had to figure this leadership thing out, and he was going to give me another shot.

He actually saved me from myself. I definitely had to face the consequences and didn't get off unscathed by any stretch. I was held accountable on many levels. In addition to our internal accountability, part of our team was unionized, so I learned hard and fast what arbitration meant and felt like. I had to take responsibility for my actions and build new bridges to replace those I'd burned. It was painful and took time. I had massively eroded trust!

The union wasn't about to send any replacement workers in a hurry, based on my boss-bitch reputation. The last thing they wanted to do was say, "Oh, well, we'll send you some new blood to suck the life out of." I had to work hard to rebuild trust with the union bosses and show them I'd taken responsibility and learned my lesson. Bridge rebuilding takes time. As much as this totally sucked, it was a very necessary, impactful and humbling experience—crucially important for my leadership evolution.

When trust is eroded, it seems like it takes at least 10 times the effort to restore it. I consider myself quite fortunate to have been given a shot at rebuilding. I didn't care how bad it sucked, I had been given a second chance, and for that, I was grateful and manically committed to figuring out this leadership thing. I didn't know exactly what to do or how to do it, but one thing was crystal clear, I needed to give people a reason to want to play on my team, regardless of their union status.

#CleanSlate

It was time for me to wipe the slate clean and start over. It takes time to recruit, hire, develop, and certainly, to build trust with a new team. Once I finally hired my new team members, I worked consciously to make sure I didn't fall back into the behaviors that demoralized people and eroded trust. I was nervous and for good reason. This was a rightfully painful and challenging period for everyone, learning from and actually living through the collateral consequences of my leadership incompetence.

After the new team was on board, I called a huddle. I felt it was important for me to own up to my prior bull ride. I confessed that I had micromanaged the previous team, pointed out everything they had done incorrectly, and looked for needles in haystacks, hoping to find that one little thing that wasn't perfect. It's fair to say that I hovered over them like a drone. Furthermore, I shared that I could be temperamental, impatient, talk over people, and didn't listen very well. I was a telling manager, not an asking leader. I let the team know I didn't consider myself "fixed." I considered myself definitely aware that what I had been doing up to that point wasn't working. I acknowledged that I needed to do something different and shared my commitment to learning how to lead. #DontBeAnAss

In spite of still being somewhat gun shy and not trusting myself due to feelings of incompetence and vulnerability, which were uncomfortable and unsettling, I had this massive desire to make my boss proud. After all, he had given me another shot, and I wasn't about to screw it up the second time around. I had to learn how to connect with people at a much deeper level in hopes of building trust and had to be willing to say things like, "I'm not really sure how to fix this problem, and I need your help." Moreover, I asked for and gave my team members permission to give me feedback regularly. I wanted to know what was and wasn't working. Looking back now, this was a massive shift in mindset, trust building and teamwork, and certainly a big step for me. I asked them to make a commitment, not just to me, but to one another. I shared my vision for us as a team. I hoped we would build a work family, one that had an all-for-one mentality. I called it "Musketeer Mentality." As corny as it sounded, it was extremely powerful in supporting us in becoming a team who had each other's back. It's worth noting, I didn't lose sight of the fact that I needed to have their back first. I'm really appreciative of the help they provided me as a young, inexperienced leader, desperately in need of feedback. A necessary and bitter pill indeed. One that I wasn't always as hungry for as I should've been. I invite you to think of the term "Musketeers" as a winning sports team. I personally love the story of Norway's Olympic ski team, the Attacking Vikings—Google them; yah like that kinda Musketeers. #NoBullRides #AttackingVikings #Musketeers

The 1990s was an interesting time. Unlike today, I didn't have the internet or an abundance of books about leadership and certainly not any that I was excited about reading. I found most seemed to be written for C-suite executives, not for me. There were two books I recall purchasing—one by Stephen Covey, *The Seven Habits of Highly Effective People*, the other by Ken Blanchard, *The One Minute Manager*. Those books helped me a lot, and we started to turn our ship around #GetTools.

In a fairly short period of time, work became fun, and results started soaring. We had a great time building a strong team together. What is cool about that company was they were all about mentorship; they asked me to mentor other high potential leaders. It was an incredible honor to pay it forward and make amends of sort. They really were a fantastic company to work for, a testament to the amazing leadership of #JAllen, #Mutz, and #Butterworth. I consider myself lucky to have been a part of their team— great memories, performance, product, commitment to service and people.

The coolest change, however, was in my development as a leader. I was becoming more open, willing to be vulnerable, asking for feedback, building relationships, and remaining committed to something bigger than my own ego. Keep in mind, my ego was still pretty massive and was complemented by a large ration of humble pie, marking the beginning of my cocooning period. Making progress. No wings just yet.

As for the unions, fortunately I eventually built a very good relationship with them and would love to be able to say I became one of their favorites. I have no idea if that was the case, other than the fact that we built a partnership and bond. It was awesome. In fact, you couldn't tell the difference between my union and non-union employees. They all ran it like they owned it. The days of reaching into their pockets for their union booklets to remind me of what was and wasn't a part of their job descriptions were over. We had become one team, equally and passionately committed to collective outcomes. We worked hard and had a lot of fun. We were a well-honed high-performance team, committed to providing exceptional customer service experiences.

I ended up staying in the Chicago market for a few more years. Unfortunately for me, at that time, my company didn't own any other downtown assets. As such, my opportunities for internal promotion were really limited to other markets or the burbs. I was a Chi-town girl all-the-way, so there was no way I was going to the burbs. Eventually, I resigned, accepting a huge promotion with another downtown company. This would prove to be a disaster. Stay tuned for Lesson 2.

Today, in my current role as a leadership consultant and coach, when working with various institutions and organizations, I will often hear the comment, "We can't achieve that level of employee engagement, performance, or create that customer experience, etc. . . . because we are unionized." Well I call B.S. It all comes down to leadership and building trust, relationships, bridges, and partnering for the win-win. I won't say it's easy, especially if you have blown up a few bridges that need rebuilding. But man, is it worth it.

I can't think of a better real-world example of this today than the incredible team at Southwest Airlines. They are astoundingly successful at embracing a ONE TEAM mindset. They're approximately 85–87% percent unionized. AMAZING! They have truly broken the mold and set the bar for other organizations and institutions to follow.

#DontBeAnAss

"Get him the right gear. Rider education classes."

Michael Baer, *Why We Ride*, Amazon Prime Video, DVD, directed by Bryan H. Carroll, USA, 2013.

Over the years, I have certainly had plenty of time to reflect on my ass-like behavior back then. I try to wrap my head around what drove me to behave so poorly as a leader. I have chalked it up to a perfect storm: being young and cocky in a progressive, results-driven downtown Chicago market. Making matters infinitely worse, I overcompensated, trying too hard to prove myself. That approach didn't land right and failed to build connections. I instead built walls and loaded guns and being a female to boot, I came off like a bitch, not a leader. Cringe. In my immature and insecure mind, I believed I needed to be this way, so I'd be respected and not taken advantage of. I didn't care if I was liked or not. That was a perilous combination. I lacked maturity, competence, and confidence. I didn't know how to lead, therefore, I used force and aggressiveness and dominance to assert authority. Ridic! Not only did I almost lose my job and my home, those team members who walked out that day never came back. As such, I never had the chance to apologize. I had blown it! I was 100% responsible for my behavior. I have lived with this fact my entire career. I failed them as their leader and truly hope they all went on to better leaders, careers and opportunities. This bull ride has truly shaped me both personally and professionally. It has made me who I am today. I thank them for holding up my mirror, revealing to me how poorly I showed up for all of them.

Let's face it, when we lead poorly, it impacts our people's mental, physical and emotional state. It creates stress at work and at home. It impacts how our team goes home to their families, interacts with their communities, peers, and customers. It impacts the quality of their work, and even worse, how they feel about themselves. In the case of my bull ride, almost all of my team members were there a lot longer than I had been. I uprooted them from their lives, homes, and work-families. I even impacted the customers' experience, for those they'd cultivated relationships with over time. They left all of them behind. The impact of poor leadership is incredibly significant; it creates huge damage, which is why we, as leaders, have to get this figured out. The cost is too great!

TREASURE HUNT: #FindtheLesson

What are the parallels in your experience? Have you been on the bull or worked for one?

If so, what was the impact?

What lesson did you learn?

What will be different for you going forward?

Do you have some rebuilding and #CleanSlating you need to take care of with your team?

What's the take away for you and your team that would be most valuable from this lesson?

Have you really looked into your leadership mirror? What would you learn if you did?

Lesson 1 #Rehash:

1. #ExpandYourTribe
2. #NoBullRides
3. #Ciao4Now
4. #NotYourMothers-LeadershipBook
5. #BadassLeader
6. #LivetoLead
7. #ThrillsandAgony
8. #BullRide
9. #HumblePie
10. #ThisBrands4U
11. #CooksCorner
12. #LikeLayerCake
13. #Stacks
14. #12Lessons
15. #Hashtags
16. #Rehashing
17. #OutsideBoxes
18. #TakingRisks
19. #BeingDifferent
20. #NotSameSame
21. #LessonsInStories
22. #Bust
23. #BombDiggity
24. #WinkWink
25. #Cheers
26. #SpeedHashing
27. #GoWithTheFlow
28. #EnjoyTheRide
29. #Different
30. #RuhRoh
31. #Suckit
32. #EmbracetheSuck
33. #CleanSlate
34. #DontBeAnAss
35. #NoBullRides
36. #AttackingVikings
37. #Musketeers
38. #GetTools
39. #FindtheLesson
40. #CleanSlating

What comes to mind is this quote by one of my favorite Badass Leaders, Simon Sinek from his incredible TED Talk based on his book, *Start With Why: How Great Leaders Inspire Everyone to Take Action*. "Leading is not the same as being the leader. Being the leader means you hold the highest rank, either by earning it, good fortune or navigating internal politics. Leading, however, means that others willingly follow you—not because they have to, not because they are paid to, but because they want to." This quote by Simon reminds me of my post bull ride epiphany. I didn't know exactly what to do or how to do it, but one thing was crystal clear, I needed to give people a reason to want to play on my team. This is the lesson embedded in Don't Be an Ass!

In order to have any hope of ever getting close to creating this, it required me to: Stop. Drop. Take a Selfie!

LESSON 2:

STOP. DROP. TAKE A SELFIE!

LESSON 2
STOP. DROP. TAKE A SELFIE!

#KnowYourSelfie

"Go at it and make sure you do it the best that you can possibly do it, so that
you're proud of what you've accomplished!"

Josh Hayes, AMA Superbike Champion, *Why We Ride*

The word "Selfie" doesn't sound very badass, but it really is, if we're willing to take a hard look at our Selfie. It takes guts to look into the mirror, to understand ourselves as leaders.

The focus of this lesson is about taking a time out. Stop. Drop. Learn about yourself. Taking a Selfie stresses the vital importance of understanding yourself, what's working for you as a leader, and even more importantly, what isn't. In the case of my bull ride, it was my absolute lack of self-awareness that was my ultimate undoing. I was oblivious to the impact I was having on others. I actually thought I was doing a great job, and that was what created the bull ride in the first place. Without being self-aware, you don't know what you don't know, so how the hell are you supposed to be able to fix what's not working? Remember, as far as I was concerned, on paper at least, we were winning. But relative to human capital casualties, it was a bloodbath. This is how bad leadership can remain undetected for excruciatingly long periods of time. They get results in spite of their lack of badass-ness. Unfortunately, this happens all too often with leaders who are utterly clueless when it comes to understanding their impact on people and performance. I was one of those leaders. The first step for me in making sure I didn't allow history to repeat itself with a new team required me to start with my mirror, my Selfie. #MyMirror

I was oblivious to my blind spot and to the emotional wake that I created for others. I was unaware and unconscious of the residual and the collateral damage my leadership style created with my body language, tone of voice, and my inward focus. That is a terrifying revelation.

Here is an example of my typical bull ride phase behavior: I would come in to the office in the morning, may or may not say, "Good morning," march into my office, a busy, self-important leader. Eye roll. More ass. Less leader-like. I'd pull reports, come out of my office and start firing off questions and barking orders. "What about this? Have you done that? This is what I want you to do." I was wound up and tense. I even walked and communicated aggressively.

First, I needed to understand myself and the impact I created. This became a huge focus for me. I tried to be present, pay attention to my team's body language, listen to their tone, slow down, stop, appreciate them, acknowledge, connect, and ask questions. It is never easy to admit we're the problem, but it is always easier to fix ourselves than someone else. I still look back and wonder, how I could be so unconscious as a leader?

There are a few indicators when there's a leadership problem:

- higher team turnover
- absenteeism
- customer service complaints
- bad social media reviews
- unproductive conflict
- higher stress levels
- worker comp claims
- missing targeted objectives

These symptoms need a proper diagnosis. I always recommend starting with the leader. If you're interested in digging into your leadership Selfie, start with asking for feedback. Consider investing in executive coaching. It's not just for the white-collar folks—just find the right one or let us hook you up with one of our Badass Coaches. Most importantly, be curious, pay attention, understand the culture you're creating for your team—get intimate with your leadership Selfie. There's an abundance of resources available. One resource I leverage consistently with leaders and teams is the Everything DiSC® profile. MDR Coaching & Consulting, Inc. are Authorized Partners for Everything DiSC®, and for good reason (www.mdr4you.com). #SameSame #ButDifferent

The answer really lies in understanding our mirror. Investing in increased self-awareness is critically important for developing our leadership strengths. It takes a certain level of fearlessness to confront and really seek to understand what is working with respect to how we communicate. Communication is a skill set that is critical for us as leaders. Many leaders really suck at this, and DiSC® will help.

#WakeUp

Even still, I understand it can be difficult for some people to look into the mirror and take a Selfie. In my case, it actually took my bull ride for me to wake up. If my team hadn't taken a stand, who knows how long I would have gone on creating that type of collateral damage and destruction?

Unlike my bull ride days, today, there are many resources available to learn about ourselves. We all need to discover as much as we can about how we communicate. Surround yourself with people who will give you sugar-free feedback. Be brave, ask courageous questions, and seek to understand your Selfie. Don't wait until you have a bull ride and create human capital casualties, or maybe even lose your job, suffer lawsuits, or destroy your reputation. If your office or department has a revolving door out front due to team turnover, I've got news for you, it's you. Stop blaming anyone or anything else—your team, your mirror, your results, your Selfie.

In extreme cases, when left unchecked, poor management skills can put your company out of business. Especially given today's socially connected climate, the damage can be catastrophic. It's important to understand you are responsible for the emotional wake you leave behind. You need to get out there and leverage resources to learn as much as you can now to elevate your Badass Leader game.

Just think about the impact oblivion can wreak. Have you ever worked for a #BadBoss who's oblivious or didn't care about the emotional wake they left behind? Let's face it, it sucks. There have been times throughout my career, when I've worked for even worse, a narcissistic boss. It is brutal. Clearly, they are not leaders. This can be incredibly challenging, especially if you're in middle management and the narcissist is at the senior executive level. This creates a tragically toxic culture and being a middle manager can be incredibly challenging when you have to sift through garbage coming down from the top. This is not just destructive; in most cases it is a no-win situation. The lesson I learned from working for a boss who lacks self-awareness, or more unforgivably, gets off on bullying or intimidating employees, is to get out fast, before it damages your reputation and you wind up with a stain on your resume for having been associated with that type of toxic leadership. #ExitStageLeft

The first job I accepted after my Chicago bull ride was working for such a narcissist. It was a mind-blowing experience. In my interview, this boss seemed almost meek and kind. It was a total rope-a-dope, and I was the dope. When I landed this promotion, I was beyond excited. I had a beautiful office, with a view of Lake Michigan, in a stunning 60-story skyscraper, on the spectacular lakefront of downtown Chicago. Oh, and my apartment was a corner-facing, 900-square-foot, one-bedroom, with an epic view of the Chicago skyline. I was flyinghigh; it was total badass. #Penthousing #NotReally #ButClose

My very first day on the job, I attended the weekly sales meeting, conducted by Mister Meek and Kind himself. I don't think I lifted my jaw off of the table the entire meeting. I was mortified. I couldn't believe the way he treated his people. This had been my first encounter with a narcissistic boss, and I was honestly sickened, and thought, "what the hell have I gotten myself into?"

Immediately after the meeting, I requested a face-to-face with him and his business partner. I voiced my concerns and let them know that I wasn't okay with being part of a team who treated people like that. I told them I'd made a mistake in joining their team. They were warm and fuzzy again, and very apologetic, reassuring me it wouldn't happen again, that this was a one-off. I was still young, dumb, gullible, and honestly, hopeful. Not wanting to give up that corner apartment and amazing opportunity so quickly, I took them at their word. Everybody has a bad day, right?

Initially, their behavior improved, and like a fool, I started to actually believe that maybeeee, it was a one-off encounter after all. As the weeks went by, I was getting to know my new team. But, I could see, hear, and feel their fear, the lack of trust, and the mounting anxiety as team meeting times approached. It was a B.S., artificially harmonious, toxic environment. Dammit, I was going to have to give up that epic apartment after all. #Sigh

Surprise, surprise. The day finally arrived, and he did it again. It was like something out of a movie. He was such an ass, definitely not a badass. He treated his team horribly. And now, I was supposed to go out there and clean up the emotional mess he just made and motivate this team to achieve their performance goals. Truly asinine.

I had seen enough. It was my turn to #ExitStageLeft. I was convinced this exec needed a checkup from the neck up. He was mentally and emotionally abusive to his people. Stick a fork in me. I was done.

So, I did it, in the middle of his tirade. I stood up, took my office keys, and slid them gently but purposefully all the way down the conference table, where they landed in his lap, and said, "I'm out. I'm not doing this. This is not who I am, and it's not who want to be associated with." I quit on the spot. I informed management that they would have the keys to my residence within seven days. It's the only time in my life I've ever walked out on the job without giving proper notice.

To this day I'm proud of what I did. I was fortunate to find a job immediately, and I moved out within seven days as promised. I went to work for a great company, where I had a very smart and kind leader, #MarkSup, who treated people wonderfully. He let me run the business like I owned it. He was a breath of fresh air. We built an awesome team and oversaw a very diversified asset with a lot of challenges. We were successful at immediately impacting both service and performance. #GameChanger

#BullyBoss

Motorcyclists used to have a very bad reputation.
"Pretty much, you were considered an outlaw."
Arlen Ness, *Why We Ride*
Fortunately, that's no longer the case.

I'm sure many of you may have experienced a few challenging bosses of your own, hopefully not the narcissistic types. And, you better not be one. Even years later, I worked for bosses who were belligerent, created fear and uncertainty, and some were even abusive. Passive–aggressive is always fun, too.

Perhaps they believed somehow their behavior would positively impact performance results. I really don't get that mindset. In fact, what it impacted was my commitment, health, sleep, personal life, and how I felt about going to work every day.

During these ass-for-a-boss times, my anxiety would kick in the day before my scheduled work day, especially if we were falling short of our goal. I wondered what the next day was going to be like, who would be publicly humiliated this week, me, or one of my peers? This type of culture does not create sustainable improvement. It fosters toxic environments and artificial harmony versus a collaborative problem-solving opportunity. How much better would our collective outcomes have been, if we could have approached our challenges by collaboratively exploring options and opportunities to support each other's goals, seeking to understand what didn't work by creating a safe environment where teams share challenges, group think and contribute to collective wins versus competing with one another? Hmmmm, now there's an idea. #NotRocketScience

During these times, my focus was keeping the target off my back and having a Plan B. After my bull ride experience and even later in my career working for a few asses myself, I understood firsthand the impact I had on my team. I implicitly identified who I didn't want to be or work for moving forward, and as a result, it took my Badass Leader commitment to a whole new level. I needed to navigate myself out of that situation and into another opportunity that could align me with a leader who held the same values I did when it came to people. Many of us have heard before, people don't leave organizations, they leave bosses—just like when my team left me.

I guarantee you, if you are an ass for a boss that is exactly the type of Plan B focus you're creating—outward on other opportunities, not inward on your business and certainly not on supporting your success.

So, what else is in it for you, should you decide to invest in understanding your Selfie? We cannot truly bring out the best in others, if we don't fully understand our mirror first. It begins and ends with us. There are massive benefits you can enjoy from really knowing and managing your Selfie and developing your Badass Leader skills. It gives you more opportunities to elevate your career. Let's face it, leaders who are successful at building winning teams have an abundance of potential for growth and advancement. It allows you to scale your businesses and create space for you to cultivate your own development. This is one of Stephen Covey's Seven Habits. If you're interested, it's Habit #7 Sharpen the Saw, from his book, *The Seven Habits of Highly Effective People*. When I Sharpen the Saw, I sleep better and am less stressed, and therefore, show up better as a leader. When there's a Badass Leader at the top of any team, the "impossible becomes possible," part of a popular quote by Chris Bradford, best-selling author from the U.K.

#InvestinYourSelfie

If you're ready to get to know your Selfie and would like to know where to start, here is a summarized 4-step approach.

Step 1

Take an Everything DiSC® Profile assessment, either Workplace or Management. I suggest DiSC® over other assessments for the same reason as the CEO of MDR Coaching & Consulting, Inc., I invested in becoming an authorized partner. It is an adaptive testing tool, meaning the test adapts to the test-taker, whereby increasing accuracy of results (Google adaptive testing if you would like to learn more). Plus, DiSC® is simple to understand and easy to immediately implement. There are some free ones out there, but don't cheap out, invest in the real deal DiSC®. You'll know it's the real deal because it's spelled DiSC with a little i. We sell it at MDR—just visit our website to learn more and support your first step in understanding how you communicate. https://mdr4you.com/everything-disc/disc-workplace.html

If you really wanna to take your badass learning to an even higher level, engage an executive coach for a couple of hours over the phone to walk you through your DiSC® results. It accelerates your outcomes. If that is not in the cards or budget for you yet, take the assessment, then leverage the tools through https://myeverythingdisc.com and practice, practice, practice. Again, it's not Rocket Science. Your outcomes will be based on your openness and commitment—easy-peasy. No excuses.

Step 2

After you've completed and understand your Everything DiSC® profile and feel like you are ready to take it up a notch. Step it up to a 360-degree assessment. I prefer Everything DiSC® 363, and also like DecisonWise© for the same reasons mentioned above, easy to understand and execute quickly. At this stage in the Selfie game, I would definitely recommend engaging a coach to walk you through your results and action planning (will not break the bank—we're talking 3–4 hours). Even Formula 1 drivers have coaches. What makes you think you don't need one? #EverythingDiSC363 #GetaCoach

Step 3

Keep in mind, throughout this DiSC® process, I encourage you to share your results and ask for feedback from your team, family, friends and mentors, people who will give it to you straight. The key for you is to remain hungry and open for feedback. Don't be defensive. That just holds you back from your potential. Suck it up. Remember, we are perfectly designed. Listen twice as much as you speak. #2Ears1Mouth

Step 4

If you really want to add some nitrous to your badass leader game and fast, invest in hiring a leadership coach for a series of sessions. Our Badass Leader Coaches are here for you. Or, find someone else, but definitely invest in your development; it doesn't need to be a long-term gig, but get some outside professional perspective.

Around 2007, I had my very first executive coaching experience with Patti Cain-Stanley #RaisingCain. She is awesome, and there's nothing like having someone totally in your corner, truly invested in Y-O-U. By the way, Patti was the one who originally inspired me to become a certified coach. Leveraging a coach had an immediate impact on my development as a leader. A word of caution—it's important to find the right coach, a personality and style that works for you and pushes you to be better, someone who doesn't hesitate or sugarcoat feedback. Don't look for a coach who's going to tell you what you want to hear. Look for a coach who's going to tell you what you need to hear. If you want to feel good, go get a massage. An executive coach is about growth and development and sometimes that growth and development can be uncomfortable. #CreatetheStruggle

So, what can you anticipate from this investment in terms of improved performance? Provided you're putting the feedback from your assessments and coaching into play, you're going to start to see a difference in week-over-week, month-over-month, and year-over-year performance. You'll notice changes with your team as well. Some improvements might start out more subtle than others i.e., fewer people coming in late or calling out, a reduction in workers comp claims, less employee turnover, more referrals start coming in, and employee conflicts and customer complaints become fewer and farther between. As such, you'll likely be able to explore ways to grow your revenue and foster greater consciousness around operating expenses. Bottom line, when we do a really great job as leaders who are self-aware, we can begin to cultivate a healthier culture. Our teams become more conscious and committed to outcomes. The impact is huge on both organizational health and economic performance. Healthier cultures lead to better performance.

#SelfieGaps

Once you identify your Selfie gaps, start expanding your toolbelt. #BadassToolbox

Over the years, I have assembled many tools from my experiences working with a variety of leaders, mentors and teams. I've also gathered tips and strategies from many incredible authors, several of whom I mention throughout this book. The lesson for me is recognizing the key ingredients for my recipe for success. Your ingredients will be different, and will depend on your team, the circumstances at hand, and how well you know them and your Selfie.

The starting point is the low hanging fruit. Simply put, know your Selfie.

TREASURE HUNT: #FindtheLesson

Do you understand what's working and not working for you as a leader?

Do you know your Selfie?

Where are your greatest opportunities for Selfie development? Got Gaps?

What are the biggest roadblocks impeding your ability to be a truly Badass Leader?

Who's in your network who will give you sugar-free feedback on what's working and what's not working? #GoSugarfree

---

When is the last time you invested in your badass leadership development?

What would a promotion mean to you? Your team, your family and your future?

What's possible for you?

Keep in mind, leadership is not a one size fits all approach. It requires agility and humility to motor you through Selfie-discovery. We're not done. We'll talk more about this in Lesson 4 #GetSupport.

I love this quote by artist William H. Johnsen. "If it's to be, it's up to me." It is a perfect description of our mirror—our Selfie.

Lesson 2 #Rehash:

1. #KnowYourSelfie
2. #MyMirror
3. #SameSame
4. #ButDifferent
5. #WakeUp
6. #BadBoss
7. #ExitStageLeft
8. #Penthousing
9. #NotReally
10. #ButClose
11. #Sigh
12. #GameChanger
13. #BullyBoss
14. #NotRocketScience
15. #InvestinYourSelfie
16. #EverythingDiSC363
17. #GetaCoach
18. #2Ears1Mouth
19. #CreatetheStruggle
20. #SelfieGaps
21. #BadassToolbox
22. #FindtheLesson
23. #GoSugarfree
24. #GetSupport

During your #SelfieDiscovery journey, it's important to keep perspective. Leadership is an evolution, not a destination, and it can sometimes be messy. Be diligent in asking for help, sharing your gaps and blind spots, and be vulnerable. Don't let your ego take you off course. BTW, vulnerability is a Badass Leader strength, not a weakness. I'm not talking about sitting in a circle holding hands kinda vulnerability; not that there's anything wrong with that. When I say BE vulnerable, it's simple. Admit mistakes, apologize, ask for help and input, say you don't know if you don't know. Set your ego aside and build relationships with your people. It's easier than you think. I had to get over myself and you can too. It helped me immensely. Bottom line—being vulnerable supports you in building a foundation of trust with your people, which is mission critical to building a #BadassTeam.

LESSON 3:

LET'S TALK ABOUT TRUST, BABY!

LESSON 3
LET'S TALK ABOUT TRUST, BABY!

#2TrustorNot2Trust

When I think back to my earlier experiences of trusting a leader, I can't help but be reminded of my fifth-grade teacher, Jerry Linkhart. I grew up in Redlands, California and went to Smiley Elementary School. To a fifth grader, Mr. Linkhart was the type of teacher you hoped you would not get. He seemed so scary! He had a well-known, no-nonsense reputation, and I was not looking forward to being in his class. I really didn't like school, except for recess and boy crushes of course, and quite frankly, I wasn't very good at it. I had to redo second grade.

Initially, I was terrified of Mr. Linkhart, but that didn't last long. He ended up becoming my absolute most favorite teacher of all time! I started looking forward to going to school. My grades improved. I was even awarded perfect attendance that year. He changed my relationship with learning. He challenged me. He bolstered my self-confidence. I wasn't stupid after all. I was just bored and uninspired. He created a healthy tension for performance, while making me feel safe. I trusted him. Somehow, I felt he was looking out for me and was committed to my success. He was committed to all of our success.

After moving on from Smiley, I returned periodically to visit Mr. Linkhart, even bringing my son by to meet him years later. He was the epitome of a #Badass5thGradeTeacher. He knew how to ignite possibility and hope in others and how to build trust. I have never forgotten the impact he made on me and my self-perception. #BadassLeaders shape us. He shaped me and for that I will always be incredibly grateful. Since sharing this paragraph, I'm committed to tracking him down—to express my appreciation for igniting my passion for learning and taking on challenges. Do you have a teacher or mentor you should thank? If so, what are you waiting for?

What I've learned about trust since then is that a lack of trust is a huge weakness for leaders. A lack of trust holds us back and more importantly holds our teams back. I mean let's think about this, if we fail to develop trust, our people won't be willing to be vulnerable with us. And if they're not willing to be vulnerable with us and reveal their weaknesses or learning needs, we've missed a huge opportunity to support their growth and development. Leadership author John Maxwell said, "People buy into the leader before they buy into the vision." I would add, it begins with trusting our leaders. #BuyIntotheLeader

#TrustYourLeader

Trust is mission critical for leaders. Once you have invested in and taken the time to truly understand your Selfie, putting those discoveries into practice is essential and at the heart of building trust. Trust is not my revelation. Many leaders have emphasized this and for good reason; it's at the core of team building and certainly indispensable if you ever hope to foster a coachable team.

In Pat Lencioni's awesome book, *The Five Dysfunctions of a Team*, his model for building team cohesiveness has trust at its foundation. I wholeheartedly believe trust is the platform on which every possibility is built, and it begins with the leader. Trust is what breathes life and possibility into leaders, teams and organizations. It is present at the CORE of any great team.

I also really value Simon Sinek's 2017, 12-minute TED Talk, "Why Good Leaders Make You Feel Safe." Watch it, you'll like it, he's a great speaker. That feeling of safety is derived from trusting our leaders. When I think back to my bull ride catastrophe, I never cultivated any trust with my team. They never felt safe. Not only was I not a good leader, I was oblivious to how important trust was to team work and performance. My biggest obstacle was I didn't even trust myself. That's tough when you're young, insecure, and inexperienced, and shows up differently from person to person. You can end up overplaying your hand, which does not promote building trust with your teams or peers. I know I did. Overcompensation is an unappealing characteristic and most certainly did not encourage other's confidence in me as their leader.

#TrustisGlue

"It's passion, passion fuels everything about motorcycling,
and camaraderie is the glue that holds it all together."
Brian Klock, *Why We Ride*

So how did I go about building trust and confidence with my new team? I would like to tee this up with a simple and dead-on quote by Pat Lencioni, in his book *The Five Dysfunctions of a Team*, when he says, "Teamwork begins by building trust, and the only way to do that is to overcome our need for invulnerability."

Where was this book when I needed it back then? Vulnerability, yikes. I had to learn to trust myself and get out of my own way, especially when it came to letting go of my ego. I was insecure and immature about what I didn't know. It is certainly something I'm not proud of and created a lot of collateral damage.

I am sure we all know plenty of immature and insecure men and women who are still capable of being vulnerable. It's called having humility, which was something I most definitely lacked. An absence of humility can create a vicious cycle. As long as you're incapable of being humble with your team, there is no way in hell that you can ever expect them to trust you. Hindsight is always clearer, isn't it? Trust and humility go hand-in-hand. Both of these didn't come naturally or easily for me and can be particularly difficult to master when organizational cultures reward behaviors that don't foster it. Some even pitting teams against one another or unintentionally promoting a win-lose mindset. #TrustHumility #HandinHand

Given my aforementioned personality type, being vulnerable or humble felt like being weak and unsure. It makes me think of the lyrics by Mac Davis, "Lord it's hard to be humble." Oh, yes, it is. And I was certainly proving not to be perfect in every way.

It's ironic, when I look back at my career and particularly at the leaders whom I've admired the most, humility was definitely a characteristic they all shared. #JAllen and #GMutz; #MaxFactor, #ProfessoraMG and #KBKingofHearts. Yes, nicknames—they know who they are ☺. They are just a few of the most memorable and impactful leaders who have contributed to my leadership evolution.

#BullyBoss

Not too long after my bull ride and walking out on the narcissist, I bellied up to the bar for yet another taste of my own bitter medicine. A little well-deserved karma, I guess. It was time for round two of experiencing how it felt to work for a boss I didn't trust. Not only didn't I trust him, (Notice I didn't say leader, I said boss.) he unfortunately, was not a leader. He was a power-wielding #BullyBoss.

How so, you ask? For starters, he was a tyrant. If he didn't like the way something looked or how someone interacted with him, he would outright fire them, or even worse call me and scream at the top of his voice. "I want you to fire blank! You f*n got that?" This boss churned and burned through leaders and team members at a rate I had never seen before. He had a reputation that made me seem like a pussycat doll compared to my bull ride days #Meow. This type of boss makes it really challenging to attract talent. Yah think?

So, how did I end up working for him? Especially after walking out on the previous #NarcissisticBadBoss. Well, it was slightly complicated. Cringe. I was asked by someone I sincerely respected to consider the opportunity. She, for some crazy reason, believed I could succeed in spite of the turbulent waters. I trusted her. She must have either trusted me or seen something in me I didn't. Maybe some karma had a play in it, too? I accepted her challenge for three reasons:

1. Quite simply, I trusted her.
2. I wanted to make her proud and support her. She said, "If anybody can work for him, I believe you can."
3. I like challenges. Call me crazy. OK, Krayzee!

The leader who offered me this opportunity supported, encouraged and had confidence in me. The difference with this challenge was I accepted it, eyes wide open, sugar-free, knowing it was not going to be a smooth ride, and boy it wasn't.

So off I went to work for #BullyBoss. My first day on the job I decided to get an early start to get myself organized. I popped in 4 hours prior to opening to get set up and acclimated. The offices were still closed and locked. I was working alone in my office, when all of a sudden, I heard this deep voice behind me. It was around 7:00 a.m. #BullyBoss was standing behind me and scared the crap out of me, probably intentionally. Only he knows for sure. I immediately recognized #BullyBoss from photos and quickly introduced myself, saying, "Hello, I'm Michelle, today's my first day, very nice to meet you," earnestly holding out my hand to shake his #BullyBoss ignored my hand and introduction. He immediately responded with, "What the f* have you been doing all day!?" Like a ding-dong I said, "Thanks for asking" and went on to explain, "I've been getting my desk organized and setting up my office. I'm really looking forward to jumping in and learning as much as I can." Blah, blah, blah. Obviously, I lacked training and therefore, had no idea how to communicate to #BullyBoss fittingly, so I just ended up fanning his flames. #BullyBoss just cut me off and barked out his request. It was something about a plastic bag that had become entangled high up in a tree branch, in front of the building, and he wanted it removed "f*n immediately!" He left abruptly, locking the door behind him. Where was Liam Neeson or The Terminator when I needed them? WOW, some introduction. A little over the top you might say. Perhaps it was a test, to see if I had any guts. I didn't, but I'd like to think I did. Wink-Wink.

This was just the beginning. It was a sky-is-falling, Chicken Little culture of playing executive Twister. Oddly enough, I stayed there around three years, which at times felt like twenty. I went through so much drama from #BullyBoss—firing team members on the spot for not liking something they did, didn't do or what they might have said. He was definitely high emotional maintenance. My team became wary of starting a conversation with #BullyBoss. Those who could, would often hide; they would radio each other as to his whereabouts. Everyone feared at any moment their head could be handed to them on a platter, albeit it would be a perfect f*n platter.

I am sure you're wondering, what the hell is the matter with you? Why did you stay? I chose to stay for a several reasons: Times were different for women back then, #BullyBoss-like behavior was more common than you'd think. The good news was the insanity wasn't an everyday occurrence. The majority of days were epic! Remember, I signed up for this undertaking eyes-wide-open and was determined to give it my best shot. Besides, leaving wasn't an easy decision; I cared about my team. As such, I was passionately committed to do my best to create a safe environment for them. I somehow believed I could make a positive difference. I did; I did end up making a positive difference! #MissionAccomplished

Not to be underestimated, was my heartfelt loyalty to the leader who invited me to take on this adventure. Was she right? Could I embrace the struggle? She was an extraordinary Badass Leader, a woman I trusted and loved working for and respected immensely. I understood her needs and believed I could help. For whatever it was worth, I wanted to make her job easier and make her proud. It was different for female leaders then, particularly in progressive, urban settings. She needed an ally, and I was ready to step up into that role. She had confidence in my ability to find a way to wade through the B.S. and create a team and a culture that was healthy, in spite of sporadic megalomaniac behavior at the top. So, I launched into Sh*Creek, and tried to navigate sometimes with what would seem to be no paddle or boat. It ultimately went much smoother than expected. #DontBeAnAss #NoPaddle #NoBoat #NoProblem

Smoother than expected yes, but don't expect any accolades from #BullyBoss. He was not the type of boss who made a habit of saying "thank you" or "good job." There were paychecks for that. Fortunately, we had leaders who fulfilled the responsibility of providing the atta-boys! My president and VP did that very well. I miss working with both of them.

They were amazing leaders who in spite of the sometimes-uncontrollable circumstances, managed to make us feel like we mattered and were valued. P.S. That's the secret sauce to employee engagement.

#WadingExpedition

So, here's the thing. What's most interesting about this whole wading expedition was the gift I backhandedly received from staying in Sh*Creek. What I learned from working for a #BullyBoss, someone who could be verbally abusive and unreasonable was how to say "yes" then figure out how. Instead of coming up with reasons, stories, or excuses why I couldn't do something, which was the last thing he wanted to hear. My job was to figure out how to make it happen. It didn't matter how outrageous the request might have seemed (not illegal, just unreasonable at times) #BeLikeBranson. This experience tested and developed my competency when it came to problem-solving, resourcefulness, and providing exceptional customer service. It also advanced my communication skills, built my self-awareness and ability to read people to understand how to remain outcome focused. I became adept at figuring out which pieces of the puzzle I needed to quickly solve to achieve the expected outcome. It sucked sometimes, but not all of the time. I also learned how to shelter and filter information for my team and customers. I tried my damnedest to make sure that I'd get out in front of it, so I could protect and shield my people from some of the potential B.S. created by #BullyBoss. I did my best to create a circle of safety during some of the uniquely trying conditions. Looking back, man, did it elevate my leadership, thinking and decision-making competencies and my ability to rally a team.

Don't get me wrong, I am not advocating for #BullyBosses. I am offering you a different lens to look through if you find yourself up Sh*Creek. There are still lessons you can learn from these Ass-as-Boss experiences. Fortunately, today there is much needed sensitively around behaviors previously practiced and thankfully no longer tolerated. #BullyBoss #SeekLessons

Looking back, it does irk me a bit. We weren't dealing with fire, flood, or blood. We were dealing with power-wielding #BullyBoss behavior. I am ashamed to admit we became really great at kissing the corporate ass #LipBalmRequired. I had a great team and work-family—people I cared about deeply and wanted to take care of and protect—oddly enough, it is an experience I cherish. Now you know why I have a lesson called Don't be a KissAss! Lol. #KeepTheGood #LearnfromtheBad

In spite of the corporate ass-kissing, we did have a lot of fun and created amazing results operationally and financially. Plus, during this whole escapade we had to navigate through truly one of the toughest disaster management crises I have ever experienced in my career. Thankfully our team was like lock-tight to a nut & bolt cohesive, so we managed through it together. Cohesive teams prevail. #LessonsLearned

When I ultimately resigned, it wasn't to run from #BullyBoss. I had achieved a level of cruising altitude and was actually loving my job, albeit keeping an eye on the skies for potential turbulence. I resigned for personal reasons (a divorce from #CopHusband, you'll learn more about him in Lesson 12. #BePatient). After submitting my resignation, #BullyBoss invited me into his office for the first time ever. In an earnest way, he let me know I'd done a great job. He was sincerely appreciative and asked me if there was anything that he could do to talk me into staying or help me on my way. I was dumbfounded and touched. My team and I had done a great job and learned so much through embracing the suck. I never imagined he took notice. It was bittersweet.

I left Chi-town, a city I loved with all of my heart, for personal reasons. I find myself still a little homesick for the wonderful people, food and city. It still feels like Sweet-Home Chicago to me. When we work with teams that become families, it's increasingly difficult to say farewell. Especially when we conquer what seems to be impossible and make it possible. #imPOSSIBLE #ChiTown

There is something to be said about weathering the storms, not abandoning ships, figuring out if we have what it takes to be successful, in spite of our circumstances. It certainly was an important part of my badass leadership ride. Yes, it took guts to stay, maybe mixed in with some stubbornness too, especially given how uncomfortable it could get at times. I had this internal desire to ride the tide and do my best and be the best leader I could be for my peeps. Those situations sometimes suck, but there are still lessons we can gain from these experiences. Keep in mind this was the late 90s early 2000s; it was not uncommon to have a bad or bully boss. Nowadays, I would most likely choose to exit stage left and #FindaNewShip.

By this time, I had gone through three extreme experiences in a very short period of time. I went from being an ass as a boss to working for a few. I walked away really proud of what I had accomplished and learned. I am honestly a better leader because of those experiences. I'm grateful, even though they sucked sometimes. Ultimately, the good times and teamwork outweighed all of it. #AttitudeofGratitude

Think about your history or current situation. Any similarities?

Over the years, several people have asked me how those situations impacted me. It was definitely stressful. I had a whole new reaction to Sundays and to my phone ringing. Ring-Ring equated to a pit in my stomach. God forbid #BullyBoss be on the line. It was never good news. As a team, we spent time trying to keep track of #BullyBoss's travel schedule to anticipate and hopefully avoid any potential land mines. My focus was on navigating through the suck while trying to shield my people. That is distracting and unhealthy. It took my eyes off of the business and focused them on placating the #BullyBoss political landscape. My team was great. They were a truly badass and cohesive team, who worked really well together and looked after one another—true Musketeers. I left that role with an entirely new perspective of who I wanted to be as a leader.

#TeacherWillAppear

Maybe you've been lucky up to this point and haven't had to deal with a #BullyBoss. How about a more common occurrence, leaders who are incapable of being vulnerable and/or admitting mistakes? Pretty disheartening and frustrating right? Over the years, I've even tried to give a few of these leaders constructive feedback, which takes guts. Unfortunately, they weren't open or ready to hear it. Keep in mind, I was guilty of that same closed mindset during my bull ride days. It reminds me of the saying, "When the student is ready the teacher will appear." I'm not sure who came up with that, as it has been attributed to Buddha and the Theosophists, but I do know I was not the teacher, and the student was definitely not interested in my opinion. #TrustIssues

When leaders won't be vulnerable, admit their mistakes and can't connect, teams have a really hard time trusting them. It goes right back to The Five Behaviors of a Cohesive Team™ Model based on the book *The Five Dysfunctions of a Team,* and Pat Lencioni's reason for placing trust at the foundation of a truly cohesive team. When our leaders are incapable of being vulnerable, most team members aren't going be vulnerable either. Without trust, we don't feel comfortable sharing our fears, uncertainties, or mistakes. We're likely to be more concerned about potential repercussions, than being forthcoming. This is a huge missed opportunity for leaders. There's nothing more helpful for us as leaders than learning about and understanding our teams. We can do so much with that knowledge in order to support our team's growth and development.

Does your team trust you?

Do you admit mistakes and connect with your players? #SelfEvaluate

So, what about the flipside? Working for leaders we trust? How is that experience different? I've had the luxury of working for quite a few leaders I've trusted. They made me feel safe and feedback was a two-way street. They weren't just open to feedback, they asked for it. I could be completely myself when I was trying to express how I felt about something and ask questions. I openly revealed my fears and mistakes. It was awesome! I didn't have to be anyone other than who I was and could ask for help if I felt

I needed additional training or development. I didn't have any insecurities or shame associated with not knowing something; I was hungry for knowledge, eager to learn, and willing to put in sweat equity. I felt like I had a partner who was vested in my development, which made me always willing to go the extra mile. I was committed to their success, not just my own. When teams trust their leaders, it impacts organizational health. Our cultures are healthier and have an incredible capacity for growth when a strong foundation of trust exists. In Simon Sinek's TED Talk I mentioned earlier, he went on to describe the impact that happens when people feel safe. "When the circle of safety is strong, they naturally trust each other and cooperate." When teams trust us and believe we have their best interest at heart, it creates a culture with exciting energy and possibility. There's an element of fun to getting it done. It almost doesn't feel like work. This type of culture extends beyond the numbers on margin; it's embodied in how we engage with one another, our customers, and even with our families. It's palpable and profitable. #SimonSays #CircleofSafety #VulnerableandHumble

#AmliFamily
"Motorcycles and family, it's life. They just go together!"
Jules Hawkins, *Why We Ride*

Amli Residential is a perfect illustration of an organization who creates a culture of safety. During the late 1980s to early 90s I had the remarkable fortune of being on their team. As team members we affectionately referred to AMLI as "F**AMLI**Y". It was, and I am sure still is, exactly the same today, one big, happy family. It had to do with the leadership at the top of the organization, who were essentially the heads of our Amli Family. I am proud to have been an Amli Family member. It was an experience I've grown to appreciate more and more over the years. #DontKnowWhatchaGotUntilitsGone

Later in my career, I had the privilege of working for multiple layers of leaders I trusted, and that's what I call a cultural superfecta. Real people magic happens when we have the stars align in that manner, top-down rock solid #Superfecta. Are your stars aligned? My team and I trusted, liked, and respected our leaders, which lead us to run our business like we owned it. There was an insane (in a good way) level of commitment and an absolute ownership mentality from my team. Our portfolio of assets had some of the most aggressive performance goals possible, and under the most challenging of market conditions. Those were some of the best days and memories of my operations career. I am grateful to these incredible leaders who developed and inspired us to grow, thrive, and succeed. I am so proud to have been able to be a part of those organizations and teams and to have worked for truly Badass Leaders. Without trust, we can forget about recruiting people who truly want to play their asses off on our teams. It's what was missing for me on my bull ride, and later, it was also what was present on every one of our Badass Teams. #TrustEqualsBIGGERWins

TREASURE HUNT: #FindtheLesson

Are you a #BadBoss, #BullyBoss or #BadassLeader?

How would your people answer that question?

Does your team feel safe? #CircleofSafety

Do they fear you, or do they trust you?

When you Ring-Ring, does it cause a pit in their stomachs?

Do your people know you believe in them and that you believe they can do it?

Are they willing to go the extra mile for you?

Do they want to make you proud?

How often do you say, "thank you" and "good job"?

Would they be dumbfounded it you told them they were doing a great job?

How do you build trust with them? Is there anything else you could do to build greater trust?

In what ways are you like Branson? #BeLikeBranson

In what ways have challenging circumstances made you a better leader?

Do you have a mentor or #Badass5thGradeTeacher you should call and thank?

Lesson 3 #Rehash:

1. #2TrustorNot2Trust
2. #Badass5thGradeTeacher
3. #BadassLeaders
4. #BuyIntotheLeader
5. #TrustYourLeader
6. #TrustisGlue
7. #TrustHumility
8. #HandinHand
9. #MaxFactor
10. #ProfessoraMG
11. #KBKingofHearts
12. #BullyBoss
13. #Meow
14. #NarcissisticBadBoss
15. #MissionAccomplished
16. #DontBeAnAss
17. #NoPaddle
18. #NoBoat
19. #NoProblem
20. #WadingExpedition
21. #BeLikeBranson
22. #SeekLessons
23. #LipBalmRequired
24. #KeepTheGood
25. #LearnfromtheBad
26. #LessonsLearned
27. #CopHusband
28. #BePatient
29. #imPOSSIBLE
30. #ChiTown
31. #FindaNewShip
32. #AttitudeofGratitude
33. #TeacherWillAppear
34. #TrustIssues
35. #SelfEvaluate
36. #SimonSays
37. #CircleofSafety
38. #VulnerableandHumble
39. #AmIiFamily
40. #DontKnowWhatcha GotUntilitsGone
41. #Superfecta
42. #TrustEqualsBIGGERWins
43. #FindtheLesson

It's worth repeating, badass does not mean perfect. It is about calling ourselves out on things that aren't serving us or our teams—stripping it down #LikeLukeBryan, having the audacity to be honest with ourselves about what we need to change. The earlier we figure this out, the sooner we can focus on what's most important. Our People. Period.

#NotPerfect #LikeLayerCake #LessonsStack #LukeBryan

LESSON 4:
PUT YOUR PEOPLE 1ST!

LESSON 4
PUT YOUR PEOPLE 1ST!

#People1st

"Your point of reference is always with the people that you're meeting and the place where you are."

Ted Simon, *Why We Ride*

Before we can be capable of truly putting people first, as mentioned in Lesson 3, we have to learn how to trust ourselves, build trust with others and be willing to be vulnerable. Trust's importance is not a new concept, nor is it rocket science, but that doesn't mean it's easy either. Pat Lencioni, Stephen Covey, and Simon Sinek are a few of my personal favorite trust building gurus. They have all shared how vital trust is to establishing relationships—which requires paying attention to others versus only to ourselves. In my case, vulnerability wasn't easy and didn't feel natural. It was awkward and honestly a little scary. It takes confidence to be vulnerable. It's truly a badass leadership strength. As you know, a lack of maturity and humility didn't serve me and were definite obstacles to building trust. I believe they hindered me on my mission to becoming a Badass Leader. Don't allow them to hinder you or derail you from putting your people first.

Here is a first-rate example of how to build trust with our teams. On my March 2019 flight from San Francisco, I picked up an issue of Southwest: The Magazine. There was an article called "Forever Herb," written by Matt Crossman. In it, Matt shares amazing leadership anecdotes about Herb Kelleher, the founder of Southwest Airlines. This is where I discovered this epic quote by Herb. "Show [people] that you admire, value, and love them as individuals, rather than just as 'producers.'" What a perfect way to describe Lesson 4. The article is a powerful tribute to a truly #BadassLeader. Southwest Airlines takes the cake when it comes to putting people first. Hats off to them. I will share more about their incredible examples of Badass Leadership throughout this book. We'll be sure to place the link to this awesome article on our Badass Leader blog for your learning and enjoyment. Look for #ForeverHerb. www.badassleader.com/blog

I love that quote by Herb. Years ago, I adopted a mantra attributed to #TeddyRoosevelt that really describes why Herb's example is on point. "People don't care how much you know, until they know how much you care."

These quotes serve as a reminders that our teams are more interested in knowing that we care about them, than knowing how smart we are. This was a huge ah-ha moment for me, especially since my focus had been on building my operational competency first versus building relationships. For the more macho guys reading this book, don't be too quick to dismiss this or #ForeverHerb for that matter. Find a way to have your teams know you care. This is not a chick thing. It's a leader thing. #NotJust4Chicks #BrosCare2 #Relationships1st

When I say put your people first, I'm referring to your team, your direct reports, the people who you interact with every single day. Whether you hired them or acquired them, it doesn't matter. They are all your people. Putting your people first is focused on helping that team. #People1st

So why is it so important to prioritize our people? At the end of the day, your people are the ones who are following through with processes, procedures, and guidelines. They're executing and getting results. They are creating customer service experiences and maximizing revenue for your business. Everything begins and ends with your people. This is why putting #People1st is the catalyst for maximizing people performance.

Post bull ride, it was important for me to reexamine my priorities, particularly when it came to shifting my focus from all about "me" to be about "we." For some reason the pig in the backseat of the Geico commercial just popped into my head. #Weeeee. Refocusing. My #Bullride forced me to recognize it wasn't all about me, it was about my people. I couldn't succeed without them. My priorities became learning how to take care of them, coach them, teach them, mentor and support them. By doing so, we created a team that became cohesive, collaborative, felt safe, and yet was challenged for growth. I needed to figure out who I needed to be as a leader to get people to want to play and perform on my team. To be successful, I needed to change. It was time for me to go from being a manager to learning how to become a leader, which doesn't happen overnight. #StackingLessons #Me2We #OrderACape

So, how did I get started? The first habit I remember adopting was the Golden Rule, which essentially says, treat people the way you want to be treated. That was certainly an improvement over what I'd been doing up to that point. But, there's a problem—they're not me. Years later, I discovered the Platinum Rule, which is basically, treat people the way they want to be treated. WOW. Imagine that. I refer to this as #GoingPlatinum and what a difference it makes!

Here's how to go #GoPlatinum as a leader—Focus on communicating with your people the way they like to be communicated with and treating them the way they like to be treated. In other words, lead people the way they like to be led. Follow me? This is not unlike the lessons in the awesome book, *The 5 Love Languages,* by Gary Chapman, where we love people the way they want to be loved. It sounds quite simple, but you have to be intentional about it, or you revert back to what feels most comfortable for you.

In order to do this effectively, you first have to know people well enough to know how they want to be led, communicated with, recognized, and developed. Remember, it starts with you. You first have to understand your Selfie, what's working for you, as well as what isn't. Then focus on being present and self-aware, starting with your mirror (focusing in). Once you have your mindset in place, it's time for you to get to know others and (focus out)—determine how to meet the needs of your people. #PeopleScience

Frequently I'm asked if putting people first was ever challenging for me. At first, it was, and I wasn't very good at it. I have a preference for focusing on results, and action. Therefore, I tend to challenge with enthusiasm when it comes to taking action and creating those results. Putting people over results took some effort and discipline. It's a little easier said than done. Breaking bad habits takes both patience and time. Some days it might take greater effort to manage my mouth #2Ears1MouthReminder. I'm not always perfect. I still screw this up sometimes, especially when I'm not paying attention to my behavior when I'm stressed out or over-tired. Part of being a Badass Leader is not making excuses. But taking responsibility for your messes. It's about being humble and always trying to do your best. Challenging yourself and then course correct if you step out of line. It takes some conscious effort and discipline to pull back the reins. As time goes on, you will hopefully do it less often and you'll be better at catching yourself before you push too hard or prioritize ineffectively.

#PullBackReins

The funny thing is, when I stopped making performance priority Numero Uno and actually prioritized my people, the impact on performance was incredible. For so many years I did it backwards. Learning to prioritize people over performance changed me. It was crystal clear that I had been doing my team and organization a disservice. Once I realized the impact my people could have on one another, our customers and our bottom-line performance, it became easy. I was also surprised by how exciting it was to watch my team win and achieve their greatest potential individually and collectively as Musketeers. It's like watching your favorite sports teams win. Once I got a taste of that indescribable feeling, I became manically committed to building Badass Teams. It has truly been a labor of love. It's my WHY. It fills me up. Yep, my drug of choice. Think of prioritizing people like coaching your favorite sports team. Who do you need to be to take them all of the way to the podium, and ultimately to winning the championship? #PeopleOverPerformance

#FeelSafe

"I get to reach into the soul of the athletes and the racers, and, you know,
feel what they're feeling hopefully and then transfer that onto their helmet."

Troy Lee, Troy Lee Designs, *Why We Ride*

Here's another great reason why you should put your people first, it helps create that circle of safety Simon Sinek referred to in his previously mentioned TED Talk, "Why Good Leaders Make You Feel Safe." BTW, you can't B.S. your way through this, it has to be authentic or you risk eroding trust. Your behaviors, words and actions must align. In coaching, we call that being congruent. When you're congruent, and your people know you put them first, they relax into their roles, and their greatest ideas come bubbling up. They're no longer playing win-lose, nor are they behaving in a dog-eat-dog fashion. They're comfortable with one another. They become more open to coaching and feedback. It doesn't feel like intimidation; it feels like contribution. When we as teams and leaders get to that place, it ignites a dynamic that feels unstoppable. Like the song by Marvin Gaye and Tammi Terrell, "Ain't no mountain high enough, ain't no valley low enough" #BoomShakalakaBoom. "A company is stronger if it's bound by love rather than by fear." Attributed to Herb Kelleher once again. #ForeverHerb #ABrosKindaLuv2 #NotJustforChicks

I know at various times throughout my career, I've been on both types of teams, ones where I felt it was dog-eat-dog, untrusting and insecure and those which operated like Musketeers—massive differences in scorecards. Musketeers always have the greatest possibilities to #OutPlayOutLastOutPerform.

In my current role as a leadership and team coach, I often hear clients say, "My customers come first, then my people. We are nothing without our customers. We wouldn't have any people without them." I typically respond with the following question, "Who's taking care of your customers?" Usually, that's all it takes. Most leaders and owners become open to reexamining their priorities. I am certainly not the first leader to suggest prioritizing your team over customers. However, I work with organizations every single week which prioritize their products, initiatives, cattle, and customers over their own people. So, what are your priorities, and how are they working for you? How are they working for your team?

#Musketeers

"They all have a bond, and it's a bond that they share by desire.
They are people that'll bend over backwards to help ya;
you're not going to leave a comrade on the side of the road
without offering to help 'em. Some of the nicest people I've
ever met are motorcyclists, hands down."

Various cast, *Why We Ride*

If you're not yet convinced, just wait until you see how much of an
impact prioritizing your people has on your customer reviews, referrals
and turnover. It's mind-blowing! Haven't we all experienced businesses

where we can feel the difference? It's palpable when you have a team who genuinely enjoys one another. They're happy and secure. It impacts your experience of them and of their company, products, etc.

Here is a frequent example I encounter since I fly so often. Oh, pun intended #FreqFlyer. There is a distinct difference between flying Southwest Airlines versus other commercial carriers. Southwest employees are happier, comfortable, and have permission to be themselves. You can feel how much they love their brand. They seem to like working together and connecting with me as their passenger too.

Let's face it, Southwest is not as comfortable as my free upgrades and extra leg room on many other carriers. It is fascinating though, in spite of being in a smaller seat, I have a better experience. I get off of the plane much happier than when I got on, and I'm a pretty happy-go-lucky kinda gal.

Many times, after a rigorous week of multiple conferences and packed travel schedules, my butt is pretty kicked. The team at Southwest completely shifts how I feel. That is powerful, especially since flying is often how I start and end my days. When I'm heading home to my family after a long week on the road. I feel happier stepping off a Southwest flight. It's contagious, I notice the passengers on Southwest are friendlier too. #HappyPassengers

Repeatedly, I'm asked how I'd respond to leaders who might say, "This is just touchy-feely stuff. It doesn't apply to our business, and we're not doing it. We've been doing this for a long time and have been quite successful." I described in Lesson 1 how some organizations and leaders get results in spite of themselves, what I called the "illusion of success." When I hear these statements, I am compelled to invite those leaders to look at how much that mindset is truly costing them. How much is being left on the table, lost in client attrition, make-it-rights, employee turnover, overtime, and workers compensation? Just to name a few metrics. More importantly what could be possible if they did shift their priorities? How much greater might their success actually be? #LikeHocusPocus

In a few more extreme cases, they might want to rethink their role as leaders of people. Leadership is people work, powered by a human capital engine. And, if they ever truly hope to maximize organizational health and performance, people priorities and attributes are non-negotiables. I hope organizations will take an honest look at themselves and their leadership teams and evaluate if they're really putting their people first or whether it's lip service, a slogan or vision statement without execution. Maybe it is time for them to consider rocking their talk. #RockYourTalk

Again, at Southwest they believe in letting employees be themselves. "Your People come first, and if you treat them right, they'll treat the customers right." Yet another heroic quote from Herb Kelleher. #ForeverHerb—Southwest: The Magazine, same issue

This is so powerful and dead on. And here's why: when leaders put their people first, it's an accelerator to performance outcomes and experiences. There's a slogan in the dairy industry, "Great milk comes from happy cows" which comes from the California Milk Advisory Board (CMAB), an agency of the California Department of Food and Agriculture. It's the same for humans. Happy people, happy customers, resulting in less turnover, higher revenue potential, greater word of mouth referrals, and better social media reviews. It all begins with people, your people. Kinda like #HappyWife #HappyLife #WinkWink.

#HappyCows

"You can tell a happy motorcyclist, by the amount of bugs in his teeth."
Ed Kratz Jr., *Why We Ride*

Badass Leadership is not Rocket Science, but it is #PeopleScience. If you want to change the way the marketplace sees your organization, then change the way you see and prioritize your people. Then you can focus on becoming epic coaches. Can I get a Hoorah?

TREASURE HUNT: #FindtheLesson

Do you have #HappyCows?

How about #HappyPassengers?

Do your people know you care?

Have you created a Circle of Safety? #SimonSays

Is a lack of maturity or humility an obstacle for you?

Do you prioritize people over performance?—Do you need to reexamine your priorities?

In what ways do you, or can you, create a Musketeer Culture?

Do you speak to people the way they like to communicate? #PlatinumStyle If so, #Shazam! If not, what do you need to do differently?

Lesson 4 #Rehash:

1. #People1st
2. #BadassLeader
3. #ForeverHerb
4. #TeddyRoosevelt
5. #NotJust4Chicks
6. #BrosCare2
7. #Relationships1st
8. #Weeeee
9. #Bullride
10. #StackingLessons
11. #Me2We
12. #OrderACape
13. #GoingPlatinum
14. #PeopleScience
15. #2Ears1MouthReminder
16. #PullBackReins
17. #PeopleOverPerformance
18. # FeelSafe
19. #BoomShakalakaBoom
20. #ABrosKindaLuv2
21. #OutPlayOutLastOutPerform
22. #Musketeers
23. #FreqFlyer
24. #HappyPassengers
25. #LikeHocusPocus
26. #RockYourTalk
27. #HappyWife
28. #HappyLife
29. #WinkWink
30. #HappyCows
31. #FindtheLesson
32. #SimonSays
33. #PlatinumStyle
34. #Shazam!

Gotta love this comment from the book, *How Google Works* by Eric Schmidt. In it he poses this question, "The world's best athletes need coaches and you don't?" I would add, our people need coaches too. And. What a perfect role for us to fulfill as their leader. If coaching has not been your thing up to this point, do what I did, hire a badass executive coach to get you there. Ain't no shame in this leadership game. #UrAnAthleteofPeople

LESSON 5:

BE AN EPIC COACH!

LESSON 5
BE AN EPIC COACH!

#EpicCoach

"If you have a sense of destiny, don't let anything stop you from making it a reality!"

—Dave Barr, *Why We Ride*

From the same Southwest Magazine article, mentioned earlier, I unearthed this epic quote by Herb Kelleher, "Southwest's essential difference is not machines and 'things.' Our essential difference is minds, hearts, spirits, and souls." When this is the mindset at the top of an organization, it's no wonder Southwest is leading the pack against all of their competitors.

Being a leader is being a coach, and if you ever hope to be successful in building and sustaining a truly #BadassTeam, it is critically important that you learn how to coach. In his book *Laws of Leadership,* John Maxwell describes in the chapter titled, "The Law of Addition," "I believe the bottom line in leadership isn't how far we advance ourselves but how far we advance others. That is achieved by serving others and adding value to their lives." That's a perfect definition of what it is to be an epic coach, *facilitating advancing others.*

When I think of what it is that makes a coach epic, Phil Jackson from the Chicago Bulls and the LA Lakers come to mind. BTW I am not much of a fan of basketball, however, I am a fan of the Zen Master himself. I identify with coaching as an active sport. It's play-by-play. It's not only sitting in the meeting room reviewing the tapes after the game. There is a time and importance in doing just that. However, an epic coach is also actively involved in and giving feedback on-the-fly—play-by-play. It includes calling timeouts, benching people, changing-up the strategy, creating the struggle or the stretch at the right time. It's exhilarating!

A badass leader becomes an epic coach when you truly know yourself first, what's working and what's not working, and what you need to do differently. You should not hesitate to get the support needed, which might involve finding a mentor or even hiring your own epic coach to help develop your coaching skills. It also takes knowing your team, their strengths and gaps, and what support looks and feels like for them.

To amplify this, you need to know how they learn and communicate and what their behavioral tendencies are. Most importantly, how do they like to be coached? What floats their boat? What motivates them and stresses them out? You need to individualize your coaching. Understand your people on an individual basis and then cross-pollinate their talents with other team members. Leverage your players and hold them high. It's important to see them in their greatest potential and coach to that. As I mentioned earlier, coaching is an active sport, and being a leader is being a coach. If you truly hope to be successful in building and sustaining a #BadassTeam, it is critically important that you know how to coach—#PlatinumStyle.

When I think of the EPIC coaches I've had in my life, they had smarts and hearts in common. They knew exactly how to connect, what to say, when to say it, and most importantly, how to say it. When working for them, I didn't just feel like an employee, I felt like a member of the tribe. Guys, this is not just chick stuff—it's like bros stuff too. When epic coaches at the top of organizations have this stuff dialed-in, it's like #RocketFuel for a performance engine.

What else did these Epic Coaches have in common?

- They cared about their people—had their backs.
- They built trust with their teams—like the pit crew and driver kinda trust.
- They were committed to developing others and building a path for growth—winning.
- They provided platinum, timely, authentic feedback.
- They held their people to their greatest possibilities—beyond how they viewed themselves—they saw their people on the podium.
- They invited weigh-in and asked for feedback—collective input, not top-down.

#GoodOl'Days

"The difference between being a passenger and being a rider is everything!"

Taye Swing, *Why We Ride*

I wasn't always an epic coach, when I was a young mid-20 something manager, I would hold information or knowledge very close to the vest, the good ol' scarcity mentality. Ridic! In my experience, guys, girls #SameSame. When it comes to vest holding, mine stemmed from insecurity—definitely not Badass Leader behavior. Insecurity is unattractive professionally as much as it is personally, and it does not serve us.

Instead of focusing on developing my replacements and building my bench strength, I was thinking my close-to-the-vest approach provided greater job security. Again, a very unhealthy quest for self-importance and very small-minded indeed. What's even worse is admitting that I actually used to enjoy the line outside of my door. As crazy as that sounds, it fed my preposterous ego. I guess in some way according to the lens I was looking through, it made me feel like I mattered, was important and needed. It provided me with the illusion of job security, which was foolish and dangerous. That unhealthy approach stifles people development and limits everyone's performance potential, self-included.

One day, years later, an epic coach said something to me along the lines of, "If you want me to support your request for a promotion, you'd better hire, train and develop your replacement." WHAAAAT? That was an eye-opener for me. Here I go again, approaching my job security the wrong way. Did I mention these lessons could also be frustrating and humbling?

Bench-building becomes even more essential for you as your role, responsibilities, and businesses change, evolve and grow. Higher stakes require more focus around grooming your replacement and cross-training your teams to ready them for advancement. Keep your departments, teams and organizations scalable. Keep in mind, sometimes your boots are not easy to fill. Many times, your company knows that, so you'd better clone yourself and build a Badass Team that can sustain your promotion or even departure—a team who will grow by your example and take the business to the next level. That's the mark of a truly epic coach and badass leader.

Developing other leaders is the greatest and most powerful value you can provide to your organization. In my case, I went from thinking small, to focusing on developing others. Let's face it, big fish/small pond might feel great, but it doesn't pay great or offer you an opportunity to grow your team and your business. Note to Selfie—Strive for #BiggerPond.

My leader journey has been a great ride, credited to many mentors and leaders along the way. There is no doubt, I didn't always recognize my coach's contributions in real time, but their impact on my ride has been life-changing, not in a sappy way, but a #BadassLeader kinda way.

Pack your saddlebags with this:

- Always build your #BenchStrength—Um, we're not talking bench press.
- Leverage the talent around you—Don't go it alone.

- Know the strengths of your team—If you don't, you'll never get as far.
- Cross-pollinate and have your team members develop others. Why do all of the work?
- Ask way more often than you tell. #NotetoSelf #BuyDuctTape
- Listen twice as much as you speak. What did you say? (Hint: 2 ears, 1 mouth for a reason) Underutilized EPIC design.

Pedal to the Metal Badass Tip:

My Blindspot. For whatever reason, I felt like I needed to appear to be the smartest person on my team and have all the answers, which was total B.S. I wasn't and didn't. So, my mindset was, why should I help anyone else? That's plum crazy talk. If you currently think that, here's my advice, knock it off; it's not serving you. #PlumCrazyTalk #NotServingU

The best method for accelerating organizational growth and opening doors for greater leadership opportunities is by developing others. Coach, train, groom your replacements, then move onward and upward. If your organizations don't recognize your epic coaching strengths, you're possibly not with the right organization. Consider finding a new racetrack. #NewRaceTrack

Keep in mind, coaching can, at times, be frustrating. You might get rubbed, from a few closed-minded drivers, but those are minimal in comparison to the impact you'll have on so many. Focus on the latter. The few are not the ones you want to define yourself by, so lace up your red Puma Ferrari racing shoes and hit the gas Baby. Have you noticed I have gone from motorcycles, to ships and now race cars? Is this called flow? I'm not really sure being a rookie writer and all? Or, maybe I just need to take my vintage 94-Fire Engine Red Miata out for a spin? #VroomVroom

#MoreSmilesPerMile

*"The role of a leader is not to come up with all the
great ideas. The role of a leader is to create
an environment in which great ideas can happen."*
Simon Sinek

Start with Why: How Great Leaders Inspire Everyone to Take Action
#SimonSays

I love what Apple's Steve Jobs said in a 2010 interview posted on YouTube called "Steve Jobs talks about managing people." "We hire great people so they can tell us what to do." Pat Lencioni refers to this as "weigh-in." Simon Sinek, Steve Jobs, and Google in similar ways refer to it is as cultivating environments where the best ideas win. In fact, Google maintains a practice for hiring "Smart Creatives." I love that name, don't you? I'd love to be known as a Smart Creative Author and Coach—has a nice ring to it. HA! The cultures they describe foster a stratosphere where teams can do their best work—environments that encourage and inspire collaboration. This is not pie-in-the-sky! This is a game changing, winning strategy where ownership mentalities thrive. It takes trust, humility, and guts to make it happen. I'm not suggesting you take a backseat on your business—quite the contrary. It's all about innovation, getting out of the weeds, and inviting your people to share their ideas, their voices and run it like they own it.

Here is another way Southwest encourages an ownership mentality. I think I'm a groupie for Southwest Leadership, don't you? As opposed to focusing on policies and procedures, their philosophy is to offer "guidelines." In 2017, their beloved founder, Herb Kelleher shared this during an interview with San Antonio Public Library. "Guidelines for leaders: These are only guidelines, feel free to break them in the interest of our customers." In spite of not ever having had the pleasure of working for Herb I have always been the type of employee, and later a leader, who operated with a guideline philosophy. Herb would have appreciated that initiative. I also love this quote by Coach Wooden. "Be interested in finding the best way, not in having your way." #BestWayNotYourWay #RunitLikeWeOwnIt

The best advice I have for leaders who are seeking resources for their development as coaches is to:

- Tap into leaders you admire, who have successfully built #BadassTeams around them. Ask them if they'll mentor you.
- #ExpandYourTribe and Join the Club on our website at https:// badsssleader.com. We are just getting started.
- Don't let your ego interfere with your possibilities. I did and for too long.

Regardless of who you ask for support, make sure it is someone who's going to challenge you—a coach who will go to bat for you and be a #BatAss for you. Choose someone who will hold up your mirror and provide you with authentic, timely feedback, to help you get out of your own way and evolve as a leader and a coach. The key for you is to stop and listen, don't defend or explain—be grateful for the feedback. #AvoidtheBullride #2Ears #EpicDesign

#BatAss

So, what's it like to work with a coach? The first time I worked with a business coach the timing was life-saving. I had a ton of responsibility headed my way, another huge startup. We were growing at an extremely rapid pace, and I needed to scale-up very quickly. Our head count was growing almost month-over-month, as were our customer counts. I needed help. The coach we hired was outside of our organization #RaisingCain— she was my very own executive coach. #AllAboutMe

After our initial 4-hour in-person meeting, we set up 55-minute weekly calls. She was my trusted advisor. I could tell her anything—what was stressing me out, keeping me up at night, my fears and wins. It's nice to have a neutral third party to confide in. It was finally all about me. LOL, it really was, and it felt great. It was a stressful time, transitioning myself and team through huge goals and rapid growth and change. I needed support above and beyond a long walk, dirt ride, or fireside chat under the stars with my sweetie and a good tequila. I definitely needed a change up—someone outside of my company and social circle to push me to the next level as an individual and a leader. Great coaches can and will do that, especially if you dig deep for a badass one. #RaisingCain did that for me.

How do you know if you're an Epic or good coach?

Here are some things to consider:

1. Team meetings are typically energetic and productive. You're not doing all of the talking, and when you do is it more asking than telling #AskvsTell. There's a healthy banter and volleying of ideas. Body language reveals a lot too. Your people aren't kicked-back, on phones or computers, or side-talking. They are physically and intellectually engaged, leaning-in, and providing productive contributions to discussions. Check out Pat Lencioni's book *Death by Meeting*. And, for even higher-velocity meetings, I love Gino Wickman's book, *Traction*. #BIGBoyPantsRequired #RedPumas

2. Teams with healthy inclusive cultures feel safe and therefore are likely to be more collaborative, resourceful, supportive and focused on collective wins. They are just chattier—in a good way for business.

3. How productive is your conflict? Are teammates engaging in healthy, hardy debates? Or, are your peeps—back alley chatting after the meeting vs. in the meeting. That is a symptom of low trust. If you need help firing up your engines, we're here for ya, check out our Badass Leader Coaching & Toolboxes on www.badassleader.com or #Callme.

4. How about team competence? Are your people being developed, cross-pollinated, and are you leveraging their strengths? Speaking of strength, how's your bench strength? There's a fantastic tool for developing team competence and avoiding the dreaded micro-managing or equally awful failure to support your team members. Check out our Badass Leader Toolbox #5 for more info or give us a #RingRing 1-800-213-0612 #Callme.

5. Do you have Happy Cows? Does your team enjoy working for you, and are they proud to represent your brand? Can you see and feel it? Can your customers see and feel it too?

6. What are your employee and client break-up ratios? How about employee and client referrals? How are you attracting new clients and employees? FYI: Word of mouth referrals are EPIC and solid!

7. How are your results given the current market conditions? Are you trending in the right direction? Are you Outplaying, Outpacing and Outlasting your comps? #OutplayOutpaceOutlast #Shazam

I would encourage you to consider investing in an engagement survey or previously suggested 360-feedback tool—these are epic coaching tools. Everything DiSC 363 ® or DecisionWise© 360 are our favs. These assessments are kind of like going to the doctor and having an executive checkup from the neck up (wink) to help you get a better understanding of how you're doing as a coaches and leader. It can be a profound and humbling experience. It's important to leverage these awesome tools sooner rather than later, to either stay the course, or course correct. Got questions? Give us a Ring-Ring. Reminder: When you decide to invest in assessments or team surveys, you always need to express your gratitude for your team's feedback. Then, be sure to share your plans of execution, and follow up and share progress with your teams. Remember, their feedback is an investment in your success. #GoodBadandUgly

#Coach

"My dad gave lessons all the time to kids all over the world that wanted to ride a bike!"

Donna Jean Kretz Forstall, daughter of Ed "Iron Man"Kretz, Sr. who won the first Daytona 200, *Why We Ride*

What's in it for you? Why invest in yourself as a coach? OMG, it's so much easier for you when you are an epic coach! Yes, at first it takes a lil' work to get our skills up to speed, but, if I had a do over, I would have become a certified coach or at least developed my coaching skills, while I was an up-and-coming team leader. That competency is invaluable for and worthy of developing. It will make your life easier personally and professionally. You will accelerate growth and development of your team and maximize their performance. #EasierThanYouThink

But wait there's more! There are so many benefits to knowing how to coach. When you develop a good reputation as a coach, you end up attracting talent who wants to come to work for you and play for your team. You will enjoy less stress and greater qualitative and quantitative outcomes with a lot less effort. Let's face it, happy teams mean fewer customer complaints. Who doesn't want less drama? When your people are happy, there's typically a favorable impact on your customers. At the end of the day, people are willing to pay more for great customer service experiences. When you get this coaching thing right, it is a game changer. To this day, I leverage and collaborate with epic coaches. We support one another on our ever evolving #BadassLeaderJourneys.

#MagicFairyDust

"The biggest thing you can do is get them the right training."

Jason Di Salvo, Daytona 200 Winner, *Why We Ride*

Many times, I hear leaders say, "I don't have time or money for this, I have a business to run." My knee jerk reaction is to say, "make time for this, create the struggle for yourself as a coach." You can't afford not to. The pay-offs are too great. Knowing how to coach saves and makes you money and opens the windows, doors, floors and ceilings for growth and earning opportunities. Besides, leadership is people work and becoming an epic coach is like magic fairy dust for building Badass Teams. #InvestInYourDevelopment

TREASURE HUNT: #FindtheLesson

How well do you know your team?

How are you leveraging their strengths and developing their gaps?

In what ways do you create #RocketFuel for your people?

Are you serving up recognition #PlatinumStyle?

How do you get your people to rally for the #BestWay instead of fighting for their way, or just following yours?

Are you listening twice as often as you speak? #2Ears1Mouth

How are you preparing for a #BiggerPOND?

How is your bench strength? Do you have people who can fill your boots so you can grow yourself, expand your role or your business?

What's one thing you can do in the next 30 days to invest in yourself to maximize your coaching skills? What else can you do? And, when?

How can, you create #MagicFairyDust for your team?

Lesson 5 #Rehash:

1. #EpicCoach
2. #BadassTeam
3. #PlatinumStyle
4. #RocketFuel
5. # GoodOl'Days
6. #SameSame
7. #BiggerPond
8. #BadassLeader
9. #NotetoSelf
10. #BuyDuctTape
11. #PlumCrazyTalk
12. #NotServingU
13. #NewRaceTrack
14. #Varoom
15. #MoreSmilesPerMile
16. #SimonSays
17. #BestWayNotYourWay
18. #RunitLikeWeOwnIt
19. #BadassTeams
20. #ExpandYourTribe
21. #BatAss
22. #AvoidtheBullride
23. #2Ears
24. #EpicDesign
25. #AllAboutMe
26. #RaisingCain
27. #BIGBoyPantsRequired
28. #RedPumas
29. #Callme
30. #RingRing
31. #OutplayOutpaceOutlast
32. #Shazam
33. #GoodBadandUgly
34. #Coach
35. #EasierThanYouThink
36. #BadassLeaderJourneys
37. #MagicFairyDust
38. #InvestInYourDevelopment
39. #FindtheLesson
40. #BestWay
41. #2Ears1Mouth
42. #BiggerPOND

LESSON 6:

BUILD A BADASS TEAM!

LESSON 6
BUILD A BADASS TEAM!

#BadassTeam

"Challenging themselves and working as a team."

Laura Klock, Land Speed Record Holder, *Why We Ride*

I find tremendous value in this powerful, yet simple quote by Pat Lencioni regarding The Five Behaviors of a Cohesive Team ™. "The single most untapped competitive advantage is teamwork." You'd think every single leader would be focused on tapping into how to improve teamwork. I don't know about you but, I'm always looking for a competitive advantage. Why not start with building your Badass Team?

In my current role, I have the good fortune of working with many organizations across multiple industries, and when teamwork suffers it can be crippling to their potential. As I've shared, what's most worrisome, is when they're successful in spite of the absence of teamwork. Imagine what could be possible, if they truly behaved like Musketeers. #Musketeers

Truly Badass Teams have a WE versus ME attitude. An all-for-one mentality doesn't happen organically; it's cultivated by us as leaders. I have often described the dynamics at play when a baseball team is on the field. With a batter at the plate, he swings, ball goes to second. I ask, what happens to the outfield? Of course, they come in to back-up second base, just in case he drops or misses it. That's Musketeer ball. Those are the behaviors you should expect to see from your players in and out of the boardroom.

A Badass Team is one which launches colossal battles for the best ideas. When Steve Jobs in the aforementioned YouTube interview spoke about managing people, he also said, "We have wonderful arguments . . . If you want to hire great people and have them stay working for you, you have to let them make a lot of decisions and you have to be run by ideas, not hierarchy. The best ideas have to win, otherwise good people don't stay." This is so true, and something I wholeheartedly advocate for and what's present on every #BadassTeam. That's badass leader scripture indeed. #WonderfulArguments

Repeatedly, I'm asked where I started in my effort to build a Badass Team. You should know by now, everything began with me, my mirror. I started with these lessons in order. Quite literally this was my ride, my journey, striving to always improve my #BadassLeader skills. #LessonsLayer #LikeYummyCake

First, there was no denying I was an ass for a boss. Hopefully you're not blind to that possibility. As you know for me, it took a massive bull ride, which forced my acknowledgement of the truth. Unfortunately, many of us remain clueless regarding behaviors that may not be serving us and others. There is nothing worse than being an ass and not knowing it. Sucks for you, them and your organization. If you're oblivious to what's not working, you will struggle to get past Lesson 1. Let's face it, you truly can't have a #BadassTeam, without being a #BadassLeader. It starts with you . . . horse first, cart second.

#HorsethenCart

So, now that you're building your #BadassLeader skills, what do you do next to support building your #BadassTeam? I love this quote by Herb Kelleher of Southwest Airlines. "We hire great attitudes, and we'll teach them any functionality that they need." #ForeverHerb #NotRocketScience #PeopleScience

When hiring, it's critically important that you set the tone and define the roles and expectations at the beginning of the interview and hiring process. My preference is to have team members be a part of the selection process as much as possible—build your tribe together. I typically describe our culture in the interview process, and it goes something like this: "If you're going to play for this team, we are an all-for-one and one-for-all kinda team. Nobody wins unless we all win. It's non-negotiable. This team has each other's back, we work through differences together and support one another's success and development. Does that sound like your kind of team?"

This is, by no means, a one and done conversation. After on-boarding, your team needs to be reminded consistently. You need to be manically committed to promoting this culture. #CulturePersonality. Sometimes it's play-by-play, day-to-day, week-to-week, month-to-month. It will vary and needs to be frequent. As their leader, you have to #RockYourTalk Or #TiltGameOver. Of course, there will be people who cross the line and violate these expectations. You can't ignore this. You have to be ready, willing and able to support a WE Culture. If you don't, you can't blame them, it's all on you. Your Team = Your Results. #Stacks

I'm frequently asked by leaders what they should do if their overarching corporate culture plays win-lose. (Notice I said if they play win-lose. I did not say if it is a toxic culture. If it's toxic, find a new boat.) Otherwise, a WE approach can survive and even succeed regardless of the greater organizational win-lose mindset. Yes, it requires more attention. Please, don't chalk it up as an excuse. Our team, our departments. Run them like we own them. Build Musketeers to maximize team success. My team leaders and I have built many Musketeer teams inside of less than stellar cultures. Granted, it's not ideal and certainly not preferred, but it can be done. Set the bar for other leaders to follow.

However, when there's a badass leadership team at the top of an organization it sets the entire organization up for success. Southwest's results speak for themselves, and have everything to do with who sits at the helm. I got a real kick out of the story Matt Crossman shared in his March 2019 article in Southwest: The Magazine the same one I mentioned earlier. He shared how Herb decided to address a branding dispute with his competitor by challenging him to an arm-wrestling match. According to this article, "A lawsuit seemed imminent. But instead of duking it out in the courtroom, Herb and Stevens chairman Kurt Herwald came up with a novel solution: an arm-wrestling competition for the rights to the slogan."

Herb Kelleher was a man of great humor and heart, who prioritized people and was understandably beloved by so many. It was a perfect example of who he was as a man and a leader. I'm not at all surprised that Southwest has remained at the top of their game. We've included a link to the March issue and article on our Badass Leader Blog—it's a great read, enjoy! #ForeverHerb #ArmWrestling https://badassleader.com

Much to the heartache of the extended Southwest family, Herb Kelleher passed away in January 2019. His legacy is sustained by the Chairman and CEO, Gary Kelly, and his incredible leadership team. In January 2019, I had the great fortune of attending Pat Lencioni's epic UnConference where Gary Kelly and Elizabeth Bryant were invited to share stories about Herb and the people culture at Southwest Airlines. It's no wonder Southwest has been profitable for over 45 consecutive years. They are the third largest carrier in the world, have over 58,000 employees, and have never laid off even one person in 24 years. They've been ranked the most admired company in the world, and even better, approximately 85% of Southwest is unionized. Now that is evidence of truly Badass Leadership. #SWBadasses

#SWLuv

"The motorcycle community is the most open, inviting community that I've ever known."

Gordon McCall, *Why We Ride*

WOW, so, how do you do that for your organization? It starts at the top of an organization, a department, a team. It starts with US. The reality is, most of the time, you don't get to hand pick your teams, you inherit them. In fact, I've had several leaders say, "I didn't get to pick or hire my team and they were "already a problem" when I came on board." My response is, great, what an awesome opportunity for you and for them. The most value you can immediately contribute to your organization is your people aptitude—what a fantastic way to put your #BadassLeader skills to work.

I would like to share an anecdote and shed some light on what's possible when leaders inherit challenging teams. I had an awe-inspiring opportunity to lead a struggling and, quite frankly, rather fragmented team. They had been coping with an ethos of defeat for a number of years. Not the same team members of course. There seemed to be a revolving door out front as well. Turnover was an issue. When I arrived, this team even looked defeated, they not only felt like a losing team, the metrics provided supporting evidence. They unfortunately were in a prolonged slump operationally, mentally and emotionally. I had the tremendous opportunity to help them help themselves by teaching them how to Weeeee. #Geico #CouldntResist

First things first. As part of the process, I had to vote a few bad swashbucklers off the island, then get to know the remaining crew. There are usually a few swashbucklers on every dysfunctional team. Show them the plank. Of course, also do all of that necessary HR stuff to make sure the Aye-Aye's are dotted.

#Swashbucklers

"So, what happened next?" Well, I couldn't do this alone. So, I recruited a few new crew members—Epic Coach #GoldenBoy, #Cillicious, and #Jules to come in as trifecta of Crew Leaders. #GoldenBoy led maintenance and customer service. #Cillicious headed up the sales team, and #Jules was the queen of policies and procedures, heading the i-dotting, T-crossing, and plank-walking departments.

It was a Superfecta of leadership, exactly what the turnaround captain ordered. My role was to chart the course for how we would succeed together #TreasureMap. Our first quest was to heal this crew and help them become #HappyPirates. This quandary wasn't created overnight, and we weren't about to fix it overnight either. The ship and the crew were in grave disrepair. Ultimately, we weathered the storms together and finally enjoyed calms seas, blue skies and smooth sailing ahead.

Approximately 18–24 months later, the crew was standing on stage, not the plank LOL. We'd discovered the treasure and were awarded booty for performance, service, audits and sales awards. The one we were most proud of was our all-hands-on-deck Crew Award. These accolades were not just internal; they were judged by our industry peers, kinda like our version of the Academy Awards. It was an honor to work alongside that amazing crew and incredible leaders. We all grew together and developed one another, and yup, we most definitely became #HappyPirates and a #HappyFamily. We couldn't have done it without every one of them, and especially without our Epic Crew Leader Coaches #Cillicious, #GoldenBoy, #Jules, and #NoSwet, our regional manager, who was our Numero Uno Badass Crew Groupie.

#BadassGroupie

"It's the interruptions that are the journey, not where you are going."

Ted Simon, *Why We Ride*

When you inherit or join teams everybody else has given up on, a team who has been unsuccessful in some way, or in some more extreme cases, even kicked to the curb. Then you go in as a turnaround leader and wade through the sh*t shows and help them discover their wins, and when they do—nothing feels better! As #BadassLeaders, it's not just our responsibility, it's an honor and a privilege.

At various points in my career, I've encountered many teams who just want to be seen, heard, and made to feel like they mattered. They wanted to be acknowledged by others who noticed that somehow their efforts made a difference. The power of acknowledgement is immeasurable. This is why leadership continues to inspire me and why I do what I do today. I love to help leaders learn how to transform teams and build healthy #BadassOrganizations. It's easier than you think. It starts with you.

This might seem like a silly metaphor and certainly not one I would attribute to the team I just described. Have you ever adopted or fostered a shelter animal? They're down and out; perhaps they have suffered abuse, neglect, or been abandoned. They feel like nobody loves them. Then one day, you walk in, love them, and provide them with a safe home. They become a part of your family. They are cared for and cared about. Maybe they're not perfect, but you train and support them and work to gain their trust. Then, one day, you see their light come back on. I have seen the lights come on for teams over and over again. You never forget that.

As a leader, you have the ability to ignite or reignite possibilities and esteem. It makes me wonder why everyone doesn't want to become a leader. When I aspired to start my own leadership development company, I wanted to do something that I would do for free if I ever won it BIG in the lottery. Leader and team development are my winning tickets #MyWhy. For me, it's about making a positive impact for others. I'm far from perfect—perfection sounds boring anyway. Again, no Rocket Scientist here—just an extremely hard-working passionate leader and entrepreneur who gets juiced on helping leaders develop more leaders. You can impact lives, families and communities. What an awesome opportunity to create a legacy. You don't need to be at the top of an organization to build a legacy. Leadership is not a title; it's a choice. #HappySailing

#HappyPirates

Let's focus on how to identify players with badass potential to join your existing crew. Here are some recommendations that can also be found on our website. We'll keep adding more as our partnerships and toolboxes expand. At a minimum, leverage the following:

1. Mindset: Know Yourself & Your Crew—remember your mirror first.
2. When replacing #Swashbucklers and hiring a new Crew, leverage the Badass Leader Toolbox Lesson11: It's an adaptive testing assessment, approved for pre-hire use. At www.badassleader.com/leadership-toolbox we've got you covered. #MDRSameSame #But-Different
3. Invest in Everything DiSC® Assessments (post hire): Awesome on-boarding, communication, Selfie and Team Building tool. Use the real DiSC®. That way you know it's the real deal. Visit our website's Toolboxes for more info. #MDRCoaching&ConsultingInc #AuthorizedPartners

4. Involve your crew members in the hiring process; let them select shipmates and build their crew.
5. If you want to go a little deeper, check out Pat Lencioni's book called *The Ideal Team Player* and the book *Start with Why* by Simon Sinek. Both are Epic reads.
6. If you're ready to take your #Badass Crew Building to a whole new level, take your team through The Five Behaviors of a Cohesive Team™ Training. #Callme #MDRSameSame #MDRCoaching&-ConsultingInc #AuthorizedPartners

This is a good place to start. Now go forth and start building the culture you and your team deserve. #HealthyOrganizations #HappyPirates

When working with varieties of teams throughout the country, I'm often asked if I have any favorite #BadassTeams or experiences. That's a tough one; it's like trying to answer which of your kids you love the most. That being said, there are certain teams who pulled extra hard on my heartstrings. Perhaps it's in part influenced by the harder the climb, the greater the love. This was a great climb. One of my proudest and most intense team experiences happened when I was working with a team in Southern California. We were responsible for starting up and overseeing the day-to-day operations for 3,000 brand new ultra-luxury residences. The property featured a sprinkling of on-site retail spaces and incredibly robust lifestyle and event programming. It was truly a kick in the pants. I absolutely loved it and my team. What an epic opportunity, team and company. #DreamTeam

This was also the toughest and most thrilling time of my corporate adventure to date. What made this climb particularly interesting was how we collectively endured some of the most uniquely challenging dynamics and circumstances I'd ever encountered. To set the table for you a little bit, we were a brand-new ultra-luxury mixed use residential development. Construction schedules had us opening a total of five developments consecutively, and some simultaneously on the same piece of dirt. In the best of market conditions, this is a cluster and stress ball to manage. Therefore, building a #BadassDreamTeam quickly was mission critical.

I'd love to take all of the credit, but it was an absolute collaborative team effort to make this happen. And happen it did! In case you're wondering, after writing that last sentence I had to stand and shake my groove thing with pride for a minute. It was truly an epic adventure in human capital performance and teamwork to say the least. #NoDreamTeam #NoSuccess

#F5

Then it happened! The forecast for the 2008 real estate market looked like an F5 Tornado; and the F didn't stand for the Fujita Scale. The 5 stood for running 5 huge projects in different phases of operation when the proverbial sh*t hit the real estate fan. YUP, the 2008 market collapse. It seemed like overnight we were faced with multiple layoffs, reduction in benefits, lower headcounts, more work, and less pay than we'd ever had before. At least we had jobs. We also had assets to run, sales performance quotas to meet, and an epic brand promise to fulfill.

This was an exceptionally stressful time for our teams, with residents coming in almost daily, giving up the keys to their dream lifestyle. They'd lost their jobs, and some lost their retirements. Many could no longer afford to pay their rent. Some began living out of their cars, and others suffered even greater heartbreaks. This was heavy emotional stuff for our teams. In real estate operations, it is not uncommon to have all of the above and more happen. When you care for people where they live, you literally see it all and then some. In my more than 30 years of experience, I have dealt with— you name it anything—including: murders, arson, suicide, death, robbery, burglary, auto theft, rapes, molestations, divorces, affairs, domestic violence, child abuse, overdoses, and celebrity mayhem. I've worked with law enforcement, including: Homeland Security, DEA, ATF, Gang Units, and Homicide. I've dealt with media relations and navigated through disasters. I can leap tall buildings with a single bound. I wish. Note to self: Order a cape from Amazon. *I need a cape.*

#GetaCape

"Handling success correctly, and handling failure."

Laura Klock: Land Speed Record Holder, *Why We Ride*

In this business, we're often first responders. We stand close to the emotional flames, which is intimate and sometimes heartbreaking. You'd think we'd be well equipped to handle this, right? We were, to a large degree, but this felt different. It was a tsunami of daily occurrences. Many of our residents had become our extended families. We had to navigate and support one another as a team, our work family. It's fascinating when we develop teams with those types of attributes, what happens is pretty cool. Your customers fall in love with you too. They refer their friends and family members. You know you're doing something right when consistently, your TOP Sources for new business are referrals. YAY Team! Our teams cultivated communities where friends became neighbors and neighbors became friends. They all became a part of our extended family. Sounds very touchy-feely, and it was. It was awesome and purposeful, and also translated in a HUGE way to margin performance.

#BadassReminder—People are willing to pay more for the emotional value and service experiences we provide—it doesn't matter what business we're in. That's what building community is all about—how we make people feel. My #DreamTeam had each other's backs and kicked ass on results—#Musketeers a family who worked hard, had fun, fought well, and developed one another. #BuildingCommunity

How are you currently building community in your role, company and/ or industry? What ideas do you or your teams have?

#RubberMeetsRoad

"You nurture it, you love it, it grows, you develop it, you restore it and then finally it's done!"

Michael Baer, *Why We Ride*

Here's the GREAT news. Lesson 6 is the Tipping Point, where the rubber meets the road, where suddenly the whole thing tips. Can I get an Amen? There are so many opportunities we have to turn around struggling teams. Challenging, challenging, yes twice, but also fun and rewarding. When leaders step in to turn around team dynamics—moving them from dysfunction to winning, sometimes it requires a different kind of cape. Depending on how much time you have to complete the turnaround, it might even require wings and a helmet.

In one particular turn-around situation, there was a need for just that. It was an interim assignment, cape, wings and a helmet recommended. With only 45 days to make an impact, we had to be fast, fearless, confident, competent, authentic and connected. Our plan was to get in hard and fast, then decelerate and level off to a nice smooth cruising altitude. It required a quick diagnostic to identify what was not working with results and operational priorities. We had a goal of quickly identifying potential root cause issues and addressing any concerns regarding team dynamics, of which there were many.

It was like team triage and operational life support focused on saving the patient—the "patient" being this team. We needed to get healthy and fast. This is an extreme true-life example. It's a good one and outlines my point around the impact you can have on teams. I hope it offers you some encouragement. A lot can be accomplished rather quickly, when you have the right approach, act authentically with confidence and guts, and maintain an outward focus. It's not about you. It's about them, your team.

#WingsRequired

I think this is an awesome metaphor for what it is to be a Badass Leader. For dirt riders, extreme hill climbing not only requires guts, it also requires speed and agility to navigate obstacles on your way through the climb—it's you against the mountain.

—Michelle's take on extreme hill climbers from the movie, *Why We Ride*

Turnarounds and takeovers can be incredibly challenging when a team doesn't know us, and in this case, I didn't have the luxury of time to build relationships. This was a short-term intervention. I had to push hard and fast to get them to hopefully choose to trust me. My modus operandi was called *Operation Push, Pull or Get Out of the Way*. Within the first 20 minutes of greeting the team as they entered the building, I presented them with three simple choices. If they were going to stay the course over the next 45 days, they would either have to (1) Push themselves and each other to get results, (2) Pull to help us get the results, or they could choose to (3) Get out of the way (meaning transfer to another team within the company a.k.a. vote themselves off of the island). I gave them about 10 minutes to decide. I shared with them that I was there to help teach them how to win as a team. It wasn't about me and my win, it was about their win. I was there to help them play like Musketeers—One Team. Sometimes teams lose their Mojo and can no longer see their greatness—our job is to help them discover it or get it back.

So, what was it like for that team? Over the years, various members have shared that they experienced a crescendo of emotions similar to my own experience. The turnaround started out kind of scary and built toward exhilarating, rewarding and confidence building. Sometimes it's necessary to make people relatively uncomfortable to have them recognize what's not working. As their interim leader, I had to quickly wake up their potential and hopefully help them create a breakthrough—and that can, at times, feel worrisome. This team was already feeling stressed and defeated. Here's what's really cool: they were all up for the challenge. In spite of how scary and uncertain it may have felt initially, they somehow chose to trust me or at least give me a shot. People want to be led, to be taught how to win and play as a team. This team wanted to be a Badass Team. Let's face it, the struggle sucks, losing sucks, and feeling like you're failing does not create outstanding results. This team was ready for the fight back onto the podium. They all were fueled by their collective desire to win. #CapesWingsandHelmets

In order to accomplish this, it was going to be mission-critical for me to #RockMyTalk. It also required empowerment from my awesome superiors, which I fully had. The key to supporting the success of this team relied on under-promising and over-delivering, helping simplify and define priorities, holding people accountable to their commitments, and praising progress. In the end, THEY did it! I didn't do it; it was their win, I just helped them see the way forward and dust off their potential.

Roughly 45 days later, we were standing in a circle, at the center of the office, toasting with champagne celebrating. It was F5 AWESOME! They did amazing things operationally in a very short and intense period of time. What I am most proud of from this scrappy team was when they became ONE team. #BuildFamilies There wasn't a dry eye in the house. I know I was ugly crying for sure, overwhelmed with pride. Come on guys I know when your favorite sports team wins you need a Kleenex too. Again, not chick stuff, winning stuff. Same people, different mindset, such powerful results—emotional #PayDirt for me.

#NewShip

There are times, however, when, in spite of doing your best as Captains, it doesn't work for some individuals on your crew. Sometimes people are victims to your feedback. Barriers to establishing or cultivating trust become obstacles for them, and that's sad and unfortunate for you and for them. In those less frequent, sucky times, perhaps it's better to pull over and invite them to find a new ship. It may be a symptom of right sailor, wrong ship or just wrong sailor? Again, be sure to cross your T's and dot your HR Aye-Ayes.

Fortunately for me those instances have been few and far between, but they have, can, and will happen, especially when you are in the early stages of building trust or in the throes of change management. It doesn't mean you are a failure; it means there are lessons. Remember, I never said being a #BadassLeader was going to be easy, or perfect. It's messy. Sometimes pushing people outside of their comfort zones can be relatively distressing. An even greater concern, in today's ubiquitous social media climate, is the fear that online blowbacks might paralyze some leaders—preventing them from growing and stretching their team's potential. Unfortunately, this can result in fostering artificially harmonious environments that are mediocre at best. Everyone's afraid of stepping on somebody's toes or offending someone. I'm not referring to jackass leaders who are abusive; that's a different conversation entirely. I honestly don't believe the teams I have led, besides the rightful victims of my idiotic bull ride years, would say I was abusive. I am talking about leaders who care enough about their team players to take a stand and challenge them when what they are doing is not serving them or the team. Again, if your team doesn't know what's not working, how will they ever improve? We all need leaders in our lives who aren't afraid to give us feedback, and we need to be badass enough to handle it. I am not perfect, nor do I want to be, however, I'm forever committed to continuing to strive to be a Badass Leader. Reminding myself when it gets uncomfortable that leadership is an evolution, not a destination.

Here's the best part, once you build your Badass Team, it is much easier to keep them being badass. When you stretch your team outside of what's comfortable, drawing out their potential, they're not only able to sustain the vision, they can even GROW it after you've moved on to #BiggerPonds. One epic coaching strategy I use to keep my #BadassTeam mentally, physically, and emotionally engaged is to make sure to provide enough variety and challenge to keep them evolving individually and collectively as a team. #CreateTheStruggle #BuildBadassTeams #EpicCoaching

TREASURE HUNT: #FindtheLesson

How would you describe #Musketeer Mentality?

Does it exist on your team? If so, kudos and keep on keepin' on! If not, what do you need to do differently to create it?

How often do your people engage in "wonderful arguments?" #SteveJobs

----

How are you ensuring the horse goes before the cart? #HorsethenCart

----

How are you handling #Swashbucklers?

In what ways is your team being a #BadassTeam?

How are you building a #WorkFamilyCulture?

What would happen if you were suddenly rewarded with a #BiggerPond?

Are you prepared?

Is your team prepared?

How do you keep your badass team engaged?

Lesson 6 #Rehash:

1. #BadassTeam
2. #Musketeers
3. #WonderfulArguments
4. #BadassLeader
5. #LessonsLayer
6. #LikeYummyCake
7. #HorsethenCart
8. #ForeverHerb
9. #NotRocketScience
10. #PeopleScience
11. #CulturePersonality
12. #RockYourTalk
13. #Stacks
14. #ArmWrestling
15. #SWBadasses
16. #SWLuv
17. #Geico
18. #CouldntResist
19. #Swashbucklers
20. #TreasureMap
21. #HappyPirates
22. #HappyFamily
23. #BadassGroupie
24. #BadassOrganizations
25. #MyWhy
26. #HappySailing
27. #MDRSameSame
28. #ButDifferent
29. #MDRCoaching& ConsultingInc
30. #AuthorizedPartners
31. #Callme
32. #AuthorizedPartners
33. #HealthyOrganizations
34. #DreamTeam
35. #BadassDreamTeam
36. #NoDreamTeam
37. #NoSuccess
38. #F5
39. #GetaCape
40. #BadassReminder
41. #BuildingCommunity
42. #RubberMeetsRoad
43. #WingsRequired
44. #CapesWingsandHelmets
45. #RockMyTalk
46. #BuildFamilies
47. #PayDirt
48. #NewShip
49. #BiggerPonds
50. #CreateTheStruggle
51. #BuildBadassTeams
52. #EpicCoaching
53. #FindtheLesson
54. #SteveJobs
55. #WorkFamilyCulture

LESSON 7:
CREATE THE STRUGGLE!

LESSON 7
CREATE THE STRUGGLE!

#HeaveHo

Storm Rider photograph taken by Michael Lichter—Look it up. It's a powerful photo that elicits feelings of riding through a storm, feeling the elements and hazards around you as you keep your head about you and navigate safely through it. Much like when we are embroiled in the suck or struggle and need to lead ourselves and our teams through to the other side.

— Michelle's Interpretation of Storm Rider photo from the movie *Why We Ride*

Let's face it, there is a reason why this quote is so well-known, "If you always do what you've always done, you'll always get what you've always got." This saying has been credited to Henry Ford and the amazing epic coach Tony Robbins. I couldn't agree more, and have therefore, learned

...embrace the struggle and opportunities that exist outside of my comfort zone. Now don't get me wrong, this has not been easy, nor is it supposed to be comfortable, but boy is it rewarding. Creating the Struggle is about striving to thrive outside of your comfort zones, to see what is possible for yourself, your teams, and your organization.

When I reflect on my life both personally and professionally, the greatest periods of growth for me have been inspired by some type of struggle. Struggle has helped me realize what I'm truly capable of, especially when I put my mind to something. It has challenged me to think differently. I've shifted from being paralyzed by the what to being hyper-focused on the how. I don't want to become complacent or even worse—uninspiring or unimpactful. I now embrace variety, change, and challenge as necessary parts of my growth too. Tony Robbins put it best during my Strategic Interventionist training, when he described his definition of one of The 6 Human Needs, "If you're not growing, you're dying."

This awesome quote by Richard Branson, is really representative of how we can create the struggle for ourselves as leaders opening up growth and possibility. "If somebody offers you an amazing opportunity, but you are not sure you can do it, say yes—then learn how to do it later." Simply put, say "yes," then figure out how. #SayYes! This has been my mantra since electing to leave the predictable comforts of corporate America to pursue my dream of becoming an entrepreneur. Now I'm not suggesting you leave corporate America. The lesson here is more about embracing the struggle and what happened to me psychologically when I no longer had a guaranteed paycheck every two weeks, a predictable environment, 401K, health benefits, bonus, and an incentive program. Not even an IT Department or any other support departments for that matter. You name it; it no longer existed. This is when every entrepreneur truly feels the impact of, the saying, "If it's to be, it's up to me!" A popular saying attributed to William Johnsen.

If I was going to have a shot at being successful as an entrepreneur, I was going to have to change a few bad habits. Prior to my departure from corporate America, I would often disqualify myself. Meaning, I wouldn't raise my hand sometimes for things because I figured I wasn't qualified to do it, or someone else was more qualified than me. Once I was an entrepreneur, I stopped disqualifying myself, and I started figuring out how qualified I was or could become. I embraced the mindset of say "yes," then figure out how. #BeLikeBranson

So, I did just that, my first huge Say YES Test happened in early 2013. I had an opportunity to respond to a request for proposal (RFP) for a massive global company. According to the minimum requirements on their request, I most definitely appeared to be unqualified across multiple areas. I decided to go for it, submit my application, explaining why, in spite of the absence of some obvious credentials, I was a fantastic choice for their consideration. I did not embellish—I gave it my very best shot!

It took me about 10 hours to complete my submittal essay. The struggle was far from over; this opportunity involved multiple challenges around creating a work product that I'd never done before. Additionally, it required me to face two of my greatest fears: flying and public speaking. JEEZ! I was stressed out and didn't sleep for days, but I was extremely focused and determined that I could DO it!

After multiple rounds of competitive interviews, evaluation of work product and presentation quality, it felt like an audition equivalent to trying out for the The Voice. I was awarded a contract. YAHOO! This epic struggle was the tipping point for me in an area of personal and professional growth. I never thought it would be possible. Yes, terrifying, but OMG, so rewarding on so many levels. I never would have imagined that only four years post-audition, I would find myself on the stage speaking in front of over 1800 people and loving it. If I would have remained in my comfort zone or continued the bad habit of disqualifying myself, my current life path would be so unbelievably different.

Here's the bottom line: be like Branson—just say Yes. The only thing worse than failure is to disqualify yourself. When I am faced with a daunting undertaking that triggers fears that no longer serve who I want to be, I often answer the question, "what's the worst thing that could happen?" Then I prepare to prevent it. I make the vision more compelling than my fear #BiggerVision. I visualize and cite a few mantras that work for me, and practice, practice, practice. I will share a few of my favorite mantras on our website at https://badassleader.com/. Build your own or leverage mine for starters.

I passionately encourage you to discover what works for you and never disqualify yourself. Instead, push yourself beyond your comfort zone, and find the opportunities to create the struggle for yourself. You'll be well on your way to realizing your undiscovered potential. Keep in mind, as a leader, it is your responsibility to embrace struggle first, setting an example for your team to follow. If you don't, you will never truly realize what is possible for you or for them. #DontDisqualify

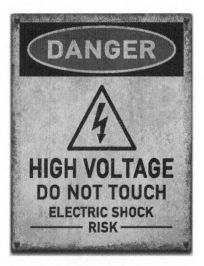

#Caution

Allow me to offer a word of caution, don't consider creating struggle for your teams, if you're not on track with Lessons 1 through 6. If you're an ass, or lack self-awareness and therefore haven't cultivated trust with your team, then, most likely you are not putting your people first. You don't get to create the struggle for them—just yet. If you prematurely jump into creating struggle for your team, you're going be viewed as an ass, and it will most likely backfire on you and compromise your desired result. I thoughtfully shared these lessons in order, based on my mistakes, to hopefully save you from your own bull ride. More importantly, absorbing these lessons will enable you to maximize your team's growth and performance potential. That doesn't mean you can't impact performance improvement if you pop the cork too soon, but it will negatively impact your credibility as a leader as well as the quality and sustainability of your results. #LessonsStack #UnconsciousCompetence

Over the years I have had frustrated bosses say (notice I didn't say leaders), "Shouldn't our employees just do what they are being told and paid to do?" My typical response to this question is, "Sure they'll do as they're told and paid to do, and you'll get what you have paid for, which is usually not their best." It will only get you so far, but it won't get you as far. I don't know about you, but I'm all about maximizing and multiplying impact to performance. Team results are a reflection of your leadership. It's important not to minimize the influence you have over the esteem and performance of your team members. If you don't believe in them, then how can you expect them to believe in themselves, or one another for that matter? Creating the struggle supports building Badass Teams when you hold individuals to a level of achieving their greatest possibility. In other words, see them in their greatest potential, not in their current reality. If you hold people low, they'll go low, and when you hold them high, they'll go higher. I am referring to challenging them beyond what they currently believe is possible, individually and collectively. Healthy, productive struggle fosters momentum, hope, possibility, and creates positive tension for performance. It's pretty awesome to witness your team stepping into their potential; and even better when they then turn to help others. Remember #FuelAdditive—like VP Racing Fuel for People. #All4One

Some examples of productive struggle creation include:

- setting almost achievable goals
- developing new skillsets
- inviting team collaboration around ideas
- solving problems making improvements
- involving them in the pirate selection process
- enabling them to run meetings and projects
- leveraging their strengths to develop others.

In other words, stretch your team outside of their job descriptions and the day-to-day monotony. Take them on the trail less traveled to develop them and discover what's possible.

#RockOn

"Never did I ever wish that the journey was over!"

Ted Simon, *Why We Ride*

A leader once said to me, "Remain in the question," which I now understand was her way of struggle creation for me. Interestingly enough, at that time during my leadership ride, I was still quite capable of being a victim to certain people, and she was definitely one of those people. She was perhaps missing a few steps needed before creating the struggle for me. Regardless, I still own how I responded to her; it's something I'm not proud of. As I've matured, I've grown to appreciate my experience with her immensely and would handle myself in a completely different way today. She ultimately made me a better leader, and upon reflection, a more successful entrepreneur. #CreatetheStruggle #DontBeAVictim #EmbracetheStruggle

Is your struggle creation building better leaders?

To understand the power and importance of these strategies, sometimes it helps if you imagine your favorite racing or sports team. How do you expect them to win, without drills, practice and challenge to help them grow as individuals and as team players? Besides, your job as an epic coach is to bring out the best in your players and team—the right kind of struggle can help them achieve previously unthought of goals.

#NotTooCalm

Here is something I've learned over the years, it's important for leaders to avoid the risk of too much stability and too little struggle. In spite of the fact that it can be comfortable and tempting, too much stability can breed mediocrity and complacency for us, our teams, and organizations. #NoMediocrity

If struggle-creating, is a struggle for you and your preference is to keep everything smooth, harmonious, and stable, you are not alone. Consider tapping into mentors, or our badass leader coaches and workshops for help. We will champion you in stretching and encouraging your team to thrive outside of their comfort zones. This will support you and them in reaching unrealized potential.

I invite you to, as my former leader would say, "Remain in the question," and ask yourself and your team, "What else should we be doing, thinking about, improving or learning?" #RemainintheQuestion #Strive2Thrive

So, what happens if you get stuck? If you are stuck in the struggle and not making progress, don't hesitate to ask for support. We all get stuck for various reasons and at various times in our lives. It took me too long in my career and life to ask for help. I learned the hard way that pride and ego are not my friends. I endured unnecessarily hard lessons as a result. The sooner you can be humble and ask for help the better for you, your team, and your company.

When I'm stuck in the struggle, here's what works for me—I say to myself, "See it for what it is, don't make it worse than it is." This prevents me from chicken-little-ing the situation. I focus on remaining grounded and not blowing things out of proportion. I find drama keeps me stuck and unproductive, and even feels disempowering. Therefore, over the years I've developed an affinity for the saying, "Save the drama for your llama." It reminds me to lighten-up, remain self-aware and to keep perspective. Again, these are rather unsophisticated rituals that work for me. Think about what will work for you—then practice. Understanding my Selfie helps. I know I have a preference for action and moving toward an empowered state. I leverage this self-knowledge by ruminating on the question, "So what, now what?" #Ask4Support #StruggleisGrowth #ChooseEmpowered

#NoDramaLlama

TREASURE HUNT: #FindtheLesson

What's the lesson for you?

How have your struggles grown you?

In what ways do you, or can you, embrace the struggle?

How are you doing on Lessons 1- 6?

Are you ready to Create the Struggle for your Team?

What struggle-creating would be most impactful for them?

What is their next BIG win?

What is #FuelAdditive for your team?

What fires up their engines?

What does your support look like to them? #StrivetoThrive #OutsideYourComfortZone

----

What would it mean for you, your business, department, organization or team to stand on the podium?

How good are you at keeping calm when the pressure is on? #NoDramaLlama

----

Who can you leverage for support?

Even professional athletes have coaches. Who can you leverage as your coach?

How can you #StayinTheQuestion?

There are times in our lives when we just have to pull up our cowboy boots and, as my good friend Paula Wittler loves to say, "Suck it up Buttercup!"

Lesson 7 #Rehash:

1. #HeaveHo
2. #SayYes!
3. #BeLikeBranson
4. #BiggerVision
5. #DontDisqualify
6. #Caution
7. #LessonsStack
8. #UnconsciousCompetence
9. #FuelAdditive
10. #All4One
11. #RockOn
12. #CreatetheStruggle
13. #DontBeAVictim
14. #EmbracetheStruggle
15. #NotTooCalm
16. #NoMediocrity
17. #RemainintheQuestion
18. #Strive2Thrive
19. #FindtheLesson
20. #OutsideYourComfortZone
21. #NoDramaLlama
22. #Ask4Support
23. #StruggleisGrowth
24. #ChooseEmpowered

LESSON 8:

SUCK IT UP BUTTERCUP!

LESSON 8
SUCK IT UP BUTTERCUP!

In the book, *How Google Works*, there's the comment, "Management's job is not to mitigate risks or prevent failures, but to create an environment resilient enough to take on those risks and tolerate the inevitable missteps." If your culture doesn't tolerate missteps (a.k.a. you can't suck it up), you won't grow players who will be capable of that either. You can't expect your team to stretch outside of their comfort zones or risk being vulnerable when you can't tolerate growing/learning pains. That puts you at risk of pouring cold water over the hot fires of your team's innovation and creativity. You'll end up extinguishing it or at a minimum, ratchet it down a few notches—and instead you will be fostering a culture paralyzed by fear. #NotetoSelfie #TolerateMissteps #NoFear

#SuckitUpButtercup is about leaders rejecting a victim mindset, and not being a wimp when it comes to self-accountability. It's about owning your commitments and facing the consequences when things don't go as planned or as hoped, or even worse, when things happen that you have no control over. Suck it up and make the best of it. We are all familiar with the saying, "It's no use crying over spilled milk." True, even if we didn't spill it. #NoCrying #SelfAccountability

As coaches, we encourage our clients to acknowledge their feelings and "experience their experience." The key is to then, move forward. At certain points in all of our lives, some things will not go as planned. If things are always going as planned, you're probably not taking enough risks. Let's face it, the suck will eventually happen. What matters most is how you navigate through the #B.S. Your team needs you to show them how it's done. The reality is, sometimes it sucks. Or you suck, the market sucks, or your boss sucks. Or maybe your personal life sucks. Such is life. Suck it up Buttercup and focus forward. #FocusForward

#NavigateThruBS

We are all familiar, with the aforementioned 2008 U.S. real estate market crisis, yep, the sh*t hit the proverbial fan. Obviously, my company, team, and I had absolutely nothing to do with it. However, we sure had the responsibility of navigating ourselves and teams through the suck. That was one of the toughest, prolonged times I have ever been through as a leader. There wasn't a lot of good news anywhere. On top of that, we had to perform scheduled layoffs of beloved team members who had become family. We cried with and for them but didn't wallow in it. We tried our very best to focus on how we could help and what we could control—our attitudes, and our commitment to compassionate service for one another and our customers. We embraced an attitude of gratitude, finding any morsels of appreciation we could scrounge up.

I worked diligently with my team leaders, to make sure we supported our team members and one another. These were truly challenging times for us all. In the midst of this chaos, we still had a massive business to run, with fewer people, but we had customers to serve, revenue to generate and bills to pay to keep the remaining team players gainfully employed and support our organization through this exceptionally challenging period. The greatest lesson during this prolonged period of difficult news was—we have to suck it up and get out there and lead our people. They're looking to us for leadership, hope, strength, comfort, compassion, and encouragement. We need to be there for them and for our customers.

Admittedly, balancing self-care and the responsibilities I had for my home and work family was not easy, but it was very important. There was not a whole lot of time to sit around licking my wounds or boo hoo-ing about what was happening in the marketplace. The best thing for us to do as a team was to work on getting a game plan together to improve our situation. The focus on helping others propelled, supported and ultimately healed us as we navigated through the suck. I remain incredibly proud of what we accomplished together during a period of intense performance and service demands. Attitude is everything!

There isn't a better representation of this point than in the awesome book by Chris Hadfield, *An Astronaut's Guide to Life on Earth*. In it, he defines the word "attitude" as follows:

"In spaceflight, 'attitude' refers to orientation: which direction your vehicle is pointing relative to the Sun, Earth and other spacecraft. If you lose control of your attitude, two things happen: the vehicle starts to tumble and spin, disorienting everyone on board, and it also strays from its course, which, if you're short on time or fuel, could mean the difference between life and death."

A paragraph later, he goes on to say:

"Ultimately, I don't determine whether I arrive at the desired professional destination. Too many variables are out of my control. There's really just one thing I can control: my attitude during the journey, which is what keeps me feeling steady, and stable and what keeps me headed in the right direction. So, I consciously monitor and correct, if necessary, because losing attitude would be far worse than not achieving my goal."

Wow, this is such a powerful description of how attitude impacts outcomes. If you hope to improve your professional altitude, you'd better learn to manage your attitude, especially if you need to get yourself and your team out of what has you stuck in the suck #AttitudeAltitude. Get the book. Read it. It's awesome. Mine was a gift from my good friend, Andrew Joyner. I cherish him and it.

#Altitude

When times are tough, it can sometimes be a little challenging to manage our attitudes. What works for me is straightforward and based on my personality preferences, so knowing myself is critically important. You might recall, I am motivated by results, action, enthusiasm, challenge, and also collaboration. Knowing that provides me with a roadmap of what I need to do in order to navigate myself away from the suck to adjust my attitude changing my altitude.

Lesson 2 comes into play here BIG time. You have to know your Selfie. If you don't know what motivates you, then how are you going to build that roadmap out of the suck? Once you get unstuck, you get to do the same for your peeps!

Find the tools that help you navigate out of the suck. Here's how I get started:

- I start by defining the suck. #DefinetheSuck
- Once I've diagnosed my current circumstances, I move to setting a goal.
    - What would success look like for me if this goal was achieved, or hurdle, pain point, or B.S. was overcome?
    - I need to remain aware of what I can control, influence, conquer, or change for the better.
- Then I start small and focus on ONE simple action.

- What is one thing I can start doing that can help or what's one thing I can stop doing?
- Next, I craft action steps that take me in the direction of my goal.

Since I know my Selfie, I know that action is an accelerator for me. Therefore, getting those action steps started is mission critical. Remaining stuck in analysis for too long can be agonizing for me which can leave me stuck.

Action is my #RocketFuel. It's the business equivalent of having your buddy attach a tow strap to your bumper to pull you out of a rut. #My4WheelLife #MotorOn

What's your #RocketFuel?

There are many awesome tools in the marketplace that can help. Find 'em. We have some in our Badass Leader Toolboxes. Check us out or give us a #RingRing, then get busy loading up your tow strap to get you out of the suck. #BuildaRoadmap #GetaTowStrap

#RocketFuel

"It became more than a motorcycle. It was a vehicle for me to take an idea about commitment and attitude and rising above, out to the world."

Dave Barr, *Why We Ride*

Victim. I don't even like the word. I admit it, over the years, I have, at times and in certain circumstances, chosen a victim's mindset—something I'm not proud of. Let's face it, choosing to be a victim sucks. It is disempowering and makes us feel terrible, as if everything is out of our control, which it isn't. When I have briefly put myself into a victim's mindset, it has been highly ineffective, extremely stressful, and a complete waste of time, energy and emotion. I would much rather focus on what I can do and dig for the lesson in it.

When you adopt a Suck it up Buttercup mindset, it positively impacts team performance and here's how: when times are tough and spirits are down, it gives you the opportunity to ask your team to be part of the solution. Invite them to collaborate on goal setting, problem-solving, and collectively designing action plans. Put their talented minds, hearts and souls to productive use to create positive change. Get them out of the rut, support them by leveraging their sweat equity to come up with the answers to overcoming the obstacle or crushing the challenge. Have them construct the very plan that's going to propel you all forward as a team. It's invigorating. It's empowering, and it can absolutely transform team cohesiveness, performance and morale! Besides, the group typically comes up with the best ideas anyway, and it gets to be their win. #OhYeah

It's important for you not to forget, the suck can be more emotional or stressful for some more than others. Every once in awhile, there will be team members, who, in spite of your coaching and supportive efforts, even shared tools and vulnerabilities, flexing and trust-building choose the route of being a victim. It sucks for you and for them. Unfortunately, a victim's mindset can sometimes spill over onto other crew members and in some #DramaLlama cases, change the vibe of an entire team overnight. If unaddressed, it can create divisions versus cohesions. It's hard on you, them and it's equally hard on the rest of the team.

There are even some team members who in spite of your best efforts can't even handle platinum style feedback intended to help improve their success and development. Even when you show that you care about them personally and professionally, for some reason, they filter that feedback in a way that's negative and, in some cases, even destructive, some even becoming litigious. Those situations are a kick in the gut and some even hurt the heart strings, especially when you're invested in and care about your peeps. It's par for the course, you're leading humans not machines; it happens. The key is, these instances need to be few and far between. If they aren't, you might need some help. You might need to buy a new mirror. #OrderNewMirror #Callme #WeCanHelp

#NoVictims

At the end of the day, it's your mirror, so start there. You are responsible for the emotional wakes you create. Different strokes for different folks.

Again, leadership isn't perfect; it's messy and the people parts can at times be complicated. What matters to me is, where my head and heart are. Are they aligned and congruent in how I lead?

So as not to leave the weight of this on just the leader, it is critically important to recognize victim behaviors early and try to help them understand the impact their mindset is having on themselves and others. Remember, if people don't understand what isn't working, how can you expect them to fix it? If warranted, I will often share my own lessons learned from my past, when a victim mindset didn't serve me. I offer coaching and support if wanted and needed. Many times, we inherit team members who haven't been coached or given constructive feedback before. Maybe they have been complained about behind their backs and never supported in recognizing the behaviors that haven't served them. Seek to understand them and their history—also make sure to get the support of your HR Team—to cross those T's and dot the Aye-Ayes. #NoVictims #Seek2Understand

So, what happens when you get derailed? How do you get back on track? I have found one powerful word to be invaluable when I'm trying to suck it up, or as my hubby and I often say, to put the cuckoo back in the clock or get the train back on the tracks—it's to #Prioritize. As a solopreneur, I am 100% responsible for keeping all of the balls in the air, pretty much all of the time. It can be an awesome challenge. It's also a common reality in the life of leaders. I'm sure many readers of this book are entrepreneurs, solopreneurs, and leaders who can relate. This being the case, I can't think of a more important skill set than knowing how and what to prioritize.

This is where the good ol' 80/20 rule applies. (Wikipedia defines it as The Pareto principle, the law of the vital few, or the principle of factor sparsity states that, for many events, roughly 80% of the effects come from 20% of the causes.) Which simply means you need to focus 80% of your energy and time on the 20% of your business that is mission critical to your success. As badass leaders you'd better be clear about what's most important, and you need to be realistic. Oftentimes, embracing the suck involves the reality that sometimes you can't get everything done as quickly as you would like. So, knowing how and what to prioritize is of game changing importance. Have you and your team prioritized what is most important together? Are you on the #SamePage? #8020 #Prioritize

#SuckitUpButtercup

In times of suck, it is important for us all to remember the hardest struggles are most likely the ones that will propel us forward, strengthen us, and make us stretch to a whole new level to discover what we're truly made of. The most badass parts of who I am today are because of my struggles. Even if at the time I didn't do such a great job of embracing the suck. I'm better, stronger and wiser both personally and professionally because of it. Therefore, I've learned to be grateful for all of it. #AttitudeofGratitude #ChangesAltitude

When you are stuck, frustrated and feeling down, and feel like the suck has defeated you, it's important to think back. I bet somewhere, somehow and in some way be it personal or professional you've probably navigated through the suck before in some aspect of your life. Therefore, you've got skills. It may not be #SameSame but that's ok. Skills are skills. Maybe you've even got the t-shirt to prove it, metaphorically speaking anyway. So, relax, see it for what it is and don't make it worse than it is—you ain't got time for chicken-little-ing. You've got people to lead. Your people are counting on you. You've so got this! #SuckitUpButtercup #SaveTheDrama4UrLlama

No duh, I'm nothing like the badass Navy SEAL and ultramarathon runner, David Goggins, or many other extraordinary individuals who have put themselves up against the most insane tests and challenges in life. I'm an everyday leader, who happens to like capes. Nothing superhero like at all, just someone who consciously makes choices to champion other #BadassLeaders, while striving to set a few badass examples for my family, my clients and organization. And, most importantly when times get tough, I take my girlfriend Paula's advice and Suck it up Buttercup!

TREASURE HUNT: #FindtheLesson

How are you at sucking it up?

Do you #TolerateMissteps?

How do you hold yourself accountable?

When was the last time you shared your mistakes with your team, or shared lessons learned and consequences?

What's your #RocketFuel?

What's your team's #RocketFuel?

How well do you know your Selfie when it comes to how you handle the suck?

What struggles have propelled you forward, strengthened you?

How have you grown as a result of the suck?

How do you handle those team members who choose to be a #Victim?

Are you a #Victim?

How do you support your team when they are stuck in the struggle?

Where do you go for support when you're stuck?

What's your #80/20?

Where should you be focused?

Where's your #DramaLlama? Is at home, or is it a roady?

How can you embrace the suck differently?

Badass Leader Tip:

Don't bring drama to work. It is the fastest way to get stuck in the suck and lose respect and credibility from your team and peers. Handle your personal life personally—and promptly ask for help when and where needed. #NoDramaZone

Lesson 8 #Rehash:

1. #NotetoSelfie
2. #TolerateMissteps
3. #NoFear
4. #SuckitUpButtercup
5. #NoCrying
6. #SelfAccountability
7. #FocusForward
8. #NavigateThruBS
9. #AttitudeAltitude
10. #Altitude
11. #DefinetheSuck
12. #RocketFuel
13. #My4WheelLife
14. #MotorOn
15. #RingRing
16. #BuildaRoadmap
17. #GetaTowStrap
18. #OhYeah
19. #OrderNewMirror
20. #Callme
21. #WeCanHelp
22. #NoVictims
23. #Seek2Understand
24. #Prioritize
25. #SamePage?
26. #8020
27. #AttitudeofGratitude
28. #ChangesAltitude
29. #SameSame
30. #SaveTheDrama4UrLlama
31. #BadassLeaders
32. #FindtheLesson
33. #Victim
34. #DramaLlama
35. #NoDramaZone

LESSON 9:
DON'T BE A KISS ASS!

LESSON 9
DON'T BE A KISS ASS!

#NoAssKissing

So, what do I mean by ass-kissing? What I'm referring to is telling people what they want to hear, instead of what they need to hear. Sometimes, it takes guts to avoid this, especially when dealing with bosses who are used to having things served up a certain way. Others may have already paved the way and conditioned your boss. Or even worse, it is embedded in the organizational culture. If that's the case, your badass communication and trust-building skills are going to need to level-up their game.

A frequently challenging situation for new leaders is learning how to balance the political power positions and egos in play at work. Sometimes we end up kissing-ass to manage or manipulate situations. That can be a slippery slope, especially if your boss gets off on your ass kissing skills. If you're not careful, you'll need to buy stock in lip balm. #NoLipBalm

I've never respected a boss who needed his or her ass kissed. They are most likely an insecure, or even worse, narcissistic leader. I have encountered a few of those types of bosses. I don't believe I was one, post-bull ride at least, but I will leave that up to my teams to judge.

Getting in the habit of ass-kissing, does not do you or your bosses any favors. I'm a huge fan of sugar-free communication. I'm not advocating for anybody to be an ass; I'm advocating for you to be honest, authentic, sincere, and respectful. Your bosses need to know what you think and why you think the way you do. They need to understand what's working and not working in the business, authentically. It is your job to deliver that message, even when it's unpopular, uncomfortable, and could in some cases, result in unfavorable or unpleasant consequences. I'm not gonna lie; there could be instances when a sugar-free approach might bite you in the proverbial ass. I have a few metaphorical teeth marks to prove it.

I was heading up a turnaround several years ago when it was time for our annual executive visit. In our business, these visits consisted of formalized inspections and meetings with senior executive team members. Simply put, the process is used evaluate how everything is running. It was still early in the turnaround efforts, and quite frankly, still in the sh*t show stage. The only thing that was running was the clock. We were running out of time to manage workloads. We were understaffed and falling short of performance expectations from a qualitative and quantitative perspective. Plus, we didn't have the operating budget needed to turn the ship around. Bottom line, we needed headcount and capital. This is never good or fun news to share. It was, however, vitally important news, especially if the turnaround efforts were going to stand a chance of being successful. I'd been trying unsuccessfully to communicate our needs and challenges, and due to the magnitude of its impact, fueled by some trust issues on my part. It was falling on deaf ears. Therefore, I made an audacious decision, some called it reckless, that I wasn't going to sugarcoat our executive visit. #Audacity #MoreAssLessBadass

When the executive team showed up, I planned to share our truth, the current reality, have them see it for what it was—and I was not about to put lipstick on that pig. Can you tell that this was not going to end well? The executive visit was on schedule. I presented the truth. I did not paint a false picture, and I did not kiss any ass. I was feeling almost righteous. Yikes! #NoWin

As the meeting came to a close, the feedback I received was on point—message received. However, I had failed on my chosen method of delivery. If I could turn back time, here's what I would've done differently. Regardless of hierarchy, I would have given the senior executive team a heads-up, so they weren't blindsided. That was my bad, my lesson learned, and I did end up creating the struggle for myself for a bit and get to own it all. It was my choice to approach the situation in that way. The executive at the time, was someone I respected. I should've informed him of my challenges in a way that didn't come across disrespectfully, which unfortunately, was exactly how it landed.

Remember this lesson, when you want to deliver sugar-free communication: it needs to always be delivered with respect, and smart timing helps too. #Respect

Badass Leaders want and need to know the truth—good, bad and ugly. How else can they support us in making a difference, improving performance, or implementing that winning strategy? You have to have the guts to step up to the plate and share your respectful viewpoint, even if you risk getting shot down. Remember the quote by UCLA basketball coach, John Wooden, "Be interested in finding the best way, not in having your way." When you choose to approach communication with this objective, you should always experience some benefit in your growth and development. #CoachWooden #FindTheBestWay

Here's a truly remarkable example of a leader for whom #NoLipBalm was expected or required. The most interesting part about this story is, it was my very first meeting with #MaxFactor. At the time he was the President of the epic company where I was working. I wish I could say my meeting with #MaxFactor was arranged to showcase the spectacular job I was doing, but in fact, it was quite the opposite and under the pressure of rather unfavorable and potentially planking circumstances.

To share an appetizer portion of backstory for context, I was hired to lead a turnaround for a struggling team and asset. It was a rough go out-of-the-gate. I believed the purpose of this meeting with #MaxFactor was for me to virtually walk the plank. From my perspective, I believed he was brought in as the #Executioner—for my last meal, I mean meeting. Perhaps it was because I believed I was on my last wooden leg HARHAR!. Or maybe it was the way #MaxFactor so eloquently introduced himself, that made me immediately feel he could not only handle the truth, he fully expected it—along with thinking "What the heck have I got to lose?"

Our 3-hour walkabout was one of the most honest, authentic, sugar-free, collaborative, thought-provoking conversations I've ever had with any leader in my career. I treasure it to this day. It was as if #MaxFactor had pulled up his chair at the dinner table, famished and starving for my perspective, the good, the bad and yes, the ugly too—and all three were served. I'm happy to report, no plank walks for me that day. I am also proud to share I didn't throw anyone overboard in the process either. I simply shared what I would do differently if it were #MyShip #MyBooty. He listened.

I am thrilled to share that the turnaround of that asset and team was incredibly successful. Thanks to an amazing team/family and to the hunger of #MaxFactor, that crew won the battle! Nothing sunk their battleship! I can't think of anything more powerful than when we as leaders are approachable, ask thoughtful questions and listen with the curiosity and hunger of #MaxFactor. I learned so much from him that day, and many years thereafter, about what it is to truly be a #BadassLeader. #NoPlankWalks #NoLastMeal

#CuriousHunger
#MaxFactor

About a year after that experience, #MaxFactor invited me to sit on a few committees for future product development. One of these projects was one I'd thrown my sword into the arena for argh-argh! This was going to be my first project meeting of its kind and would put my sugar-free communication skills to the test. I was absolutely the greenest crew member on the ship among the numerous talented senior executives from multiple disciplines. The purpose of this meeting was to review the approved architectural plans for the initial multi-phase project. Being new to this project, I was given a high-level overview.

Again, #MaxFactor showed up to this meeting curious and hungry for input #CuriousHungry. He invited my perspective in spite of the fact that I'd never been in a meeting like this, and in many respects this ship had sailed. In spite of my sea legs and because of my previous experience with #MaxFactor, I felt completely comfortable speaking up. I trusted him. I had a few questions and some comments regarding operations and the use of some designated "quarters." What happened next was cannon-blowing and a testament to his truly Badass Leadership. He was intrigued with my inquiry and commentary and directed the team to have the architects make significant changes. He then invited me to create an operations plan to chart the course for our operational success for him and the executive team. It was simply amazing!

To say I walked out of that meeting fired-up, highly engaged, and committed to designing the best operations plan I could muster up is an extreme understatement #LoyalPirate. I don't think my feet touched the water for a good two days. The operations plan and architectural changes were approved and executed with amazing success. #WalkingonSunshine #BlueSkiesAhead

Having had the incredible responsibility and privilege of opening and operating these unprecedented assets was truly one of the greatest privileges and highlights of my corporate career, which included navigating through the 2008 market bubble-burst.

This is an important take-away—when I was invited to participate in that very intimidating executive meeting, I could have made a very different choice. I could have held my ideas inside and kept quiet. Just kissed ass and told these very accomplished and seasoned executives what they expected to hear. After all, the project was absolutely spectacular, so that would have been easy. Or, I could speak up, ask questions, and take a risk in sharing my perspective. The even bigger lesson here is how #MaxFactor invited input and collaboration from his team, and especially from someone like me, most definitely a greenie in the scheme of things. He asked questions like, "What would you do differently?" It is extremely empowering when you invite weigh-in from your crew. It opens up endless possibilities. Who knows, you might even discover uncharted lands? #BeLikeColumbus

This quote by the great author, Adrian Gostick, beautifully sums up how I see captains like #MaxFactor. "Great leaders in our study treated their people like partners in the organization. That meant they created for their people a sense of connection by teaching them how their jobs impact the larger organization. And they showed them growth opportunities, how they can grow and develop with the company." #PeoplePartners

Badass Leader Tip:

First and foremost, lead like #MaxFactor. Don't be a boss who needs to have your ass kissed. Listen to your people like it's your last meal. Be hungry, open, and interested in what they have to share. Secondly, be respectfully sugar-free and authentic. Share your perspective and don't create unnecessary struggles for the sake of needing to be right. That is a violation of Lesson 1 Don't be an Ass! Lastly, just say no to #LipBalm.

TREASURE HUNT: #FindtheLesson

How do you balance the political power positions and egos in play at work?

How can you respectfully avoid ass-kissing?

How can you respectfully tell people what they need to hear vs. what they want to hear?

Are you creating a #LipBalmCulture?

If so, what can you do differently?

Would your people say you are more interested in finding the BEST way, or in having YOUR way? #CoachWooden

----

In what ways are you starving for your people's perspective? #CuriousHunger #MaxFactor

----

How can you create more opportunities for others to speak up, ask questions, and take risks in sharing their perspectives?

How are you cultivating #PeoplePartners?

If you are not developing people partners, or do not feel adept at it, what will you do differently?

Lesson 9 #Rehash:

1. #NoAssKissing
2. #NoLipBalm
3. #Audacity
4. #MoreAssLessBadass
5. #NoWin
6. #Respect
7. #CoachWooden
8. #FindTheBestWay
9. #NoLipBalm
10. #MaxFactor
11. #Executioner
12. #MyShip
13. #MyBooty
14. #BadassLeader
15. #NoPlankWalks
16. #NoLastMeal
17. #CuriousHungry
18. #LoyalPirate
19. #WalkingonSunshine
20. #BlueSkiesAhead
21. #BeLikeColumbus
22. #PeoplePartners
23. #FindtheLesson
24. #LipBalmCulture
25. #CuriousHunger

LESSON 10:

BE A GROUPIE!

LESSON 10
BE A GROUPIE!

#BeAGroupie

"If you look at the scene in Star Wars,
the bar scene, that's Bike Week!"

Gordon McCall, *Why We Ride*

I don't know about you, but when I think of the word "groupie," I envision being at my favorite rock concert like—Small Town Titans, Tool, Metallica, Colt Ford, or Aerosmith. I would be in the front row, going out of my mind in the throes of their performance, wearing the t-shirt and lining up for their autographs after the show. The band members on the stage would be able to see, feel, and even hear my adoration of them, and understand my appreciation for their artistry.

Being a groupie in the context of being a Badass Leader is all about cat-howling for your team, letting them know they rock and are badasses, praising progress and celebrating victories. Wear the t-shirt and ask for their autographs, and for God's sake #CatHowl. I don't know about you, but I've spent more time with my teams than I have with my own family, and, sure as hell, a lot more time than I have with the Small Town Titans and Metallica. Being a Groupie is like VP Racing Fuel for People. #FuelAdditive #WeartheTshirt #Autographs #PraiseProgress #CatHowl

During my bull ride days, I was a groupie for a party of one. It was all about me. Post-bull ride, I realized it was not about me at all; it was about my people. Being a groupie as a leader is about staying passionately engaged in the progress of your people. As much play-by-play as you can rally! This goes back to prioritizing your people first, understanding the most important aspect of your business is accelerating their success. That's the multiplier! You can't do that sitting on the sidelines. You have to suit up for the game called leadership and get your mind into a state of maximizing people performance. Be the best groupie they've ever had. If you're not present, then you're missing opportunities to accelerate their success. Call timeouts for high-fives, provide platinum style feedback, and listen to your people with the hunger of #MaxFactor. Acknowledge and appreciate their input. I will repeat a previously shared quote, "People don't care how much you know until they know how much you care." And that's a fact Jack. #Accelerator #RocketFuel

This is another powerful message from badass author Adrian Gostick, "The simple but transformative act of a leader expressing appreciation to a person in a meaningful and memorable way is the missing accelerator that can do so much and yet is used so sparingly." So, what the hell's the matter with us? Why is this so hard for some leaders? And why is it done so sparingly? In order for you to do as Adrian has suggested, you need to know your people and you need to be intentional about how you provide meaningful and memorable feedback. When it's done correctly, this is absolutely like racing additive to engagement, reduction in turnover, and a maximizer to performance results. The key is it has to be authentic, believable, consistent and preferably delivered platinum style. Yes, the good old platinum rule for groupie leader behavior applies—recognize people the way they want to be recognized. Understand what floats their boat when it comes to rewards and recognition. Do you know what their preferred recognition currency is? In other words, how do they like to get paid emotionally? Financially? Through prizes or otherwise? When it comes to recognition, not as many people as you might think want a bright lights, big city shindig, on stage, with a trophy. Perhaps a meaningful one-on-one conversation, private lunch, a shot of kombucha, cold brew or good tequila will do the trick. Hand written notes can be even more impactful and less traumatizing for certain personality types. It's not rocket science. It's people science, we are not machines.

#SaveWater

I love being a groupie for my people. I call them my people, not in a way that creates a monarchy. It's like describing "my people," like this Georgia-born-girl would describe her kinfolk. It's a term of endearment, #Kinfolk. I love my people like family. I am who I am because of them, and I'm responsible for taking care of them #LikeFamily. As the former turnaround magician and CEO of Ford Motor Company, Alan Mulally, would say, "I am responsible for 'loving them up!'" If you haven't discovered the book about his incredible job of saving Ford Motor Company, this former executive vice president of Boeing and CEO of Boeing Commercial Airplanes is also an inductee to the International Air & Space Hall of Fame—Yep, drop the mic, he's an official #BadassLeader. This book is a MUST read! *American Icon,* by Bryce G. Hoffman. So many Badass Leaders have led with their smarts and their hearts, and Al Mulally is a perfect example of both. #LoveEmUp. In early 2019 I had the great honor of meeting this #PeopleLegend in person. #ImAGroupie #AmericanIcon

#GroupieBoss

On a more recent trip, I was asked if I've ever had a groupie for a boss? Why, Heck YES—as I throw my cowgirl hat into the air! The first one who comes to mind is #ProfessoraMG, a former VP of mine. I affectionately refer to her as #ProfessoraMG for good reason. She was the master of many things, particularly when it came to loving-up her people and being a #BadassGroupie. She was a stark raving groupie fan for us! She not only wore the t-shirt, she designed it like Versace! The gift for you in learning about her is the same as the one she gave to those of us who were lucky enough to be voted onto her island.

Here's how this #Groupie rolls:

1. You are her number one.
2. She never lets you forget that, even when it is a sh*t show.
3. She is passionate about people and imparts her wisdom on them, hence the name #Professora. She wants to help you become the best version of you.
4. She never prioritizes performance over her people/kinfolk.

When I think of public figures who remind me of her, I immediately think of Oprah. She always makes you feel like you are the most important person in the room. She connects with people at an emotional level. Everyone falls in love with #ProfessoraMG, my team and self-included. We love #Oprah2.

When your boss is your number one groupie, you are inspired to embody the #MaxFactor. You pull up your chair, hungry to learn from them, to grow, to try something new and different and to be open to their feedback and coaching. It's a beautiful and powerful thing—symbiotic really. #ProfessoraMG #ThankU

#GroupieCulture

Here is what's really cool about being a groupie as a leader, particularly as an owner or senior executive leader. You can create an organizational groupie culture. #MassiveMultiplier

Remember #MaxFactor? How could you forget him, right? He hired an extraordinary man of smarts and heart, I call him #KBAceofHearts and #ProfessoraMG reported to him. It was a perfect people storm of groupie leaders. The goals we had as team leaders and players were MASSIVE! The tension for performance was incredibly high, BUT, when we create a #GroupieCulture, it just feels different. It's like watching the Yankees play the Red Sox—intense and exciting! Whichever uniform we're wearing, we're playing our asses off to win! That is EPIC indeed and helps us all ride the changing tides with greater skills, thrills, ease, and certainly winning outcomes. #CelebrateWins #BeGroupies

TREASURE HUNT: #FindtheLesson

In what ways are you a Groupie for your people? #GroupieBoss

When is the last time you cat-howled for them?

Would they say you wear their t-shirt? #ProfessoraMG

Can they see it, feel it and hear that you're a Groupie for them?

How do you currently praise progress and celebrate wins?

How are you creating, or can you create a #GroupieCulture?

Lesson 10 #Rehash:

1. #BeAGroupie
2. #FuelAdditive
3. #WeartheTshirt
4. #Autographs
5. #PraiseProgress
6. #CatHowl
7. #Accelerator
8. #RocketFuel
9. #SaveWater
10. #Kinfolk
11. #LikeFamily
12. #BadassLeader
13. #LoveEmUp
14. #PeopleLegend
15. #ImAGroupie
16. #AmericanIcon
17. #GroupieBoss
18. #ProfessoraMG
19. #BadassGroupie
20. #Oprah2
21. #ThankU
22. #GroupieCulture
23. #MassiveMultiplier
24. #KBAceofHearts
25. #CelebrateWins
26. #BeGroupies
27. #FindtheLesson

LESSON 11:

EXPAND YOUR TRIBE!

LESSON 11
EXPAND YOUR TRIBE!

#ExpandYourTribe

"My husband's in a motorcycle club. It's like a family.
They all know each other
and ride together, they all watch out for each other."

Taye Swing, *Why We Ride*

Expanding my tribe was most certainly an overdue lesson for me and one I needed to learn at least 25 years earlier! I have no doubt that I missed several awesome opportunities by failing to embrace this lesson much sooner. Unfortunately, this was an area where I was slow to mature, suffering from some delayed leadership development. I hope you're not guilty of the same limiting beliefs I had, and if you are, knock it off. It doesn't support you in becoming a Badass Leader, nor does it set a favorable example for others to follow. #KnockitOff

In spite of being successful at managing my team, I did not always play well with others, particularly when it came to my peers. Idiotic indeed. This is something else I'm not proud of, and happily share my lesson and the difference it made for me when I finally acknowledged the value of tribal expansion, plus, it's waaaaaay more fun to WE than to me! #GeicoYetAgain

Let's start with what didn't serve me, shall we? Obviously, I wasn't perfect in this area, nor was I very open. At times I could be cocky, defensive, protective, even combative, truly unbecoming leadership behaviors. And yes, there were times when I played win-lose with my peers. Ridiculous! I had the wrong mindset period when it came to my attitude about peer-to-peer relationships. My viewpoint was I wasn't at work to make friends. I was there to get the job done, lead my team, serve our customers, maximize performance of our assets, blah, blah, blah. This is all bullshit. Expanding your tribe is mission critical to maximizing all of those and more desired outcomes. I wasn't focused on expanding my tribe or sharing any secrets of my team's success. I was thinking small and still competing, versus contributing. Sad but true. Some of the missed opportunities were not just with my peers, I'm sure it was also with a few of my bosses' peers, the leaders outside of my vertical reporting line.

When you fail to expand your tribe and opt instead to keep only a select few members in your pipeline, it limits your potential. This ultimately impacts your team and organization's health and performance. Additionally, it doesn't encourage cross-pollination of team talent. For years, I watched peers earn promotions, and move up quickly. They had expanded their spheres of influence and had built a bench of people who could readily move into their roles. Which in turn opened up opportunities for growth for themselves and others.

As mentioned previously, it's unfortunate and true there are many organizations who either unintentionally or intentionally encourage and reward internal competitiveness, breeding a win-lose culture. A few of them even pit peers against one another. This certainly doesn't create the space to foster any tribal expansions. In those types of environments, my results-oriented, competitive personality can too easily gravitate toward win-lose, versus, a "better together" approach. Bottom-line, Win-Lose really equals Lose-Lose! #PlankingIncluded

#BuildCommunity

"When you ride motorcycles, people always say hi to each other, and you know, you don't see people who drive cars waving at everybody in the car."

Damien Doffo, Doffo Winery, *Why We Ride*

It is your responsibility as a leader to teach your team how to treat their peers and share the value and power of collaboration. Focus on building community, expanding relationships, contributing to the development of others, not just your reporting peeps. By doing this, you not only build collective competence, you foster greater connections and esteem for one another. That my fellow leaders, makes us even more valuable to our organizations and that is BADASS! When we cultivate one another—I can't even begin to describe the staggering impact this has on customer experiences, team development, revenue potential, operational effectiveness and organizational agility. It is a massive multiplier! #Cha-Ching #ExpandYourTribe

If you want to build a badass legacy, you have to show 'em how it's done—you need to #RockYourTalk and #ExpandYourTribe. This right here is a competitive advantage, not just for your team, department and organization, but for you as a leader. We are always better together both personally and professionally. And, we are certainly more capable of building a badass organization when we leverage our intellectual capital collectively.

#OneTeam
#Musketeers
#BuildCommunity
#BetterTogether
#TribalExpansion

I sincerely hope in some way my mistakes, bumps, bruises, and lessons will compel you to expand your tribe. You can start by joining the club at https://badassleader.com—it's a place where we all can connect, share lessons learned, develop, and support one another. Maybe even make some new friends and reconnect with old ones. Let's partake in epic adventures and be groupies for one another! #YouAreNotAlone #ShareStories #BeLikeGumby #ExpandYourTribe #JoinTheClub #Callme

#RockOn

TREASURE HUNT: #FindtheLesson

What are you waiting for?

_____

_____

_____

How have you expanded your Tribe?

_____

_____

_____

If not, what can you do to #ExpandYourTribe?

_____

_____

_____

Are you cocky, defensive, protective, even combative when it comes to working with peers?

_____

_____

_____

How can you set an even better example for others to follow?

_____

_____

_____

What could be possible for you and others through #ExpandingYourTribe?

How can you focus on building community, expanding relationships, and contributing to the development of others, not just your reporting peeps?

How can you build collective competence and foster greater connections and esteem for your team and peers?

How can you #ExpandYourTribe in a #WinLoseCulture? What can you do in spite of your circumstances?

How will you connect, share stories and lessons learned, and develop other #BadassLeaders? #MakeNewFriends #JointheClub #BadassLeader

----

Lesson 11 #Rehash:

1. #ExpandYourTribe
2. #KnockitOff
3. #GeicoYetAgain
4. #PlankingIncluded
5. #BuildCommunity
6. #Cha-Ching
7. #ExpandYourTribe
8. #RockYourTalk
9. #OneTeam
10. #Musketeers
11. #BuildCommunity
12. #BetterTogether
13. #TribalExpansion
14. #YouAreNotAlone
15. #ShareStories
16. #BeLikeGumby
17. #JoinTheClub
18. #Callme
19. #RockOn
20. #FindtheLesson
21. #WinLoseCulture
22. #BadassLeaders
23. #MakeNewFriends

LESSON 12:

LOVE
SOMEBODY
LIKE U!

LESSON 12
LOVE SOMEBODY LIKE U!

#LoveU

I would like to kick off this lesson with a quote from Steve Jobs' 2005 commencement speech at Stanford University. "Your time is limited, so don't waste it living someone else's life. Don't let the noise of others' opinions drown out your own inner voice. And most important, have the courage to follow your heart and intuition." #DontWasteTime

I love that quote. Speaking of love, I love my hubby, family, friends, food, good tequila, smokin' results, epic adventures, life, and being an entrepreneur. The list goes on, and on, and on. But, taking time to care for myself? What? I ain't got time for that. Honestly, that is not the right attitude whatsoever. This is my greatest area of needed focus and improvement. Much of my life has been about accomplishing life, not loving somebody like me. I am convinced it stemmed from having a father whose measurement of worth was based on what I achieved. That's a whole other book ... coming soon to an Amazon cart near you, LOL. No really, I mean it. #GarbageIn #GarbageOut #ToDoList

The lesson I would like to share in this chapter is actually a hand-me-down from my late ex-husband, Al Porrata. Unfortunately, he lost his brutal fight with cancer in 2012, at which time we'd been divorced for over 10 years #FuckCancer. Al proudly served with Chicago Police Department District 18, for 20 years, Badge #7430—#RIPThor. Al would admit the greatest gift he ever gave me wasn't his husband of the year award, it was in fact this incredible lesson. He learned this lesson and shared it with me during the last six weeks I spent with him embroiled in his final battle. Fortunately, for us both, we did heal from our history and had loving closure, before he started his last ride into the afterlife—probably on his motorcycle somewhere cruising the Milky Way.

#MilkyWay

"You're flying through space at the twist of a throttle!"

Jay Allen, *Why We Ride*

Before I share his final lesson, a little context might be helpful. Al was an overachiever. He rigorously accomplished life, had an incredible need for feeling significant and acquiring things. He somehow thought these would fulfill him and bring him joy. His priorities were to work his ass off acquiring lots of possessions, so when he retired, he would be able to share and enjoy them all and feel like he'd finally made it! During my final days with Al, he admitted he'd defined success and joy by owning houses, apartment buildings, and 16 Badass Toys. Yeah, this was his happiness. He had the pink slips and storage garages to prove it.

It is interesting how perspective changes when you're on "death row," a term Al shared with me when describing his experience of being terminal. His priorities changed dramatically, as did his definition of what it was to be happy. #DeathRowPerspective

These were Al's lessons for me that I pay forward to each of you:

1. Nothing's more important than having your health. Without it, nothing else matters.
2. There's no possession more important than those you love. Friends & Family.
3. There is nothing he wanted more, than more time for #2.

#GoodHealth #Family&Friends #MoreTimefor#2

Al shared that he really could have been much happier, if he had realized all along, that he already had everything he needed to make him happy. His possessions became of no importance to him. He would have traded everything for #1 so he could have more #2 and #3. It makes me very sad to know he died with so many regrets. He was adamant that I embrace his lessons, his greatest gift.

I feel so fortunate to have been able to share those final weeks with him, as incredibly difficult as it was to see such a strong man brought to his knees by such a relentless disease. I have embraced his gift, and it has drastically changed the way I live my life. I continue to work really hard, but now I play my ass off too. Family, friends, food, fun, and adventure are all priorities for me now. I'm passionate about savoring the journey. It's no longer only about just achieving life and seeking approval.

During this ultimate ride called life, it's vitally important that we take care of ourselves, mentally, physically, and emotionally. (I have #2 and #3 dialed-in, but honestly still have some room for improvement on #1.) Living life on the road often makes eating healthy, exercising regularly, and getting enough sleep really challenging. I know I need to suck it up buttercup and embrace my struggle. Sharing Al's lessons with all of you has invited me to reconnect with his gift. It's true, there's a notable difference in how I feel, during the times I get three-outta-three dialed-in compared to how I look and feel when I fall short—kinda like more badass vs. less badass. #AlLessons #LoveSomebodyLikeU #LiveLikeYoureDying #EnjoytheRide

TREASURE HUNT: #FindtheLesson

How are you #WastingTime?

Are you accomplishing life?

Are you taking care of yourself?

If so, #RockOn!

If not, what needs to be different for you?

What do you prioritize?

How's that working for you?

How do your priorities serve your Family & Friends? #GoodHealth
#Family&Friends #MoreTimefor#2

Are you living like you're dying? #LiveLikeDying

What can you do to #EnjoytheRide even more?

#FindTheTreasure

"Take advantage of these blessings that we've been given with our health and live 110% in the moment."

Jay Allen, *Why We Ride*

Here are some final aspirations for you:

- Wear the T-shirt.
- Ask for their Autograph.
- Enjoy the ride.
- Make a Difference.
- Rock Your Talk.
- Be a Groupie.
- Build a Legacy.
- Love Yourself.
- Love-up your People.

- Good Health and More Time for #2.
- Live to Lead.
- Love to Ride.
- Do no Harm but do U.
- Embrace the Lessons.
- Drink good Tequila.
- Go get you some Badass Wings.
- If you like this book, you'll share it.
- #ShareYourLessons2

And always remember, if you're going to be an ass, be a Badass Leader. #LeaveALegacy #Cheers2 #BadassLeaders

#1Shot4Man
#AnotherGiantShot4Mankind
#Apollo50th
#CasamigosReposado
#GoodTequila

"Tomorrow my friend, is promised to no one!"

Dave Barr, *Why We Ride*

Lesson 12 #Rehash:

1. #LoveU
2. #DontWasteTime
3. #GarbageIn
4. #GarbageOut
5. #ToDoList
6. #FuckCancer
7. #RIPThor
8. #MilkyWay
9. #DeathRowPerspective
10. #GoodHealth
11. #Family&Friends
12. #MoreTimefor#2
13. #AlLessons
14. #LoveSomebodyLikeU
15. #LiveLikeYoureDying
16. #EnjoytheRide
17. #FindtheLesson
18. #WastingTime
19. #RockOn!
20. #FindTheTreasure
21. #LeaveALegacy
22. #Cheers2
23. #BadassLeaders
24. #1Shot4Man
25. #AnotherGiant-Shot4Mankind
26. #Apollo50th
27. #CasamigosReposado
28. #GoodTequila

ACKNOWLEDGEMENTS

Thank you to you my readers, I have no idea if my story, tips and shared strategies will help you on your journey. I sure hope so, I shared them with faith that they would. I wish you much success and thank you for coming along with me on my ride and for making an investment of time and attention to learn from my lessons and struggles. Keep On Keepin' On! I invite you to visit our Badass Leader website, explore the toolboxes and most importantly I hope you'll share your lessons to help other badass leaders. #JointheClub #ExpandYourTribe #LivetoLead #BadassLeader https://badassleader.com/

Thank you to the most important person in my life, my love, and badass hubby, Robert Betke. He is my #1 Badass Groupie. He's been unbelievably supportive of my entrepreneurial adventures, unconventionality and the passionate process of bringing this book and our perfectly blended lives together, creating this epic life of love, friends and family! #CooksCorner #DTLove #MyTrueWhy #WhatMattersMost #NothingCompares2U

To all of my kids, even if I didn't carry you in my belly, I carry you in my heart and love you madly! Topanga, Nico, Zack and to my belly-born son Zach and my precious g-babies Jude and Silas. You all ROCK my heart and my world! I'm a Massive Groupie for you all and so very proud of each of you! #HappyLife #WearingtheTshirt #Groupie4U #LoveIsOurFamily #MoreTimefor#2

Thank you to my crazy, awesome family and dear friends. I have had the great fortune of having so many loved ones guide me along my personal and professional ride. I love you all like crazy and can't wait to make more food, fun and memories together! #GoodFoodVinoandTequila #GreatLaughs

#MakingMemories #LoveOurFamily #FriendsAreFamily2 #TreasureHunt #FoundMySisterJodi #Took45Years

My heartfelt thank you to Wing Lam for writing my forward. Wing is a co-founder of Wahoo's Fish Taco, which he co-owns and started with his brothers Ed and Mingo. They just celebrated Wahoo's 30th anniversary, and now serve more than 60 locations across the U.S., plus their first international location in Japan. #Amazing! I have so much respect and love for their unpretentious brand and their commitment to food, family and togetherness—truly hallmarks for a healthy life, family and organization. I love their message, "Our food is true to this experience, worldly and uncommonly delicious. We'll always offer you the best of where we've been to fuel your adventures. At Wahoo's, we encourage you to nourish yourself with food and experiences that make you feel more alive. So, ride those waves, care for your community, love what you eat every day, and be authentically you. Our family is here to feed yours." Now you understand why I asked Wing to write my forward. I value what they value both personally and professionally. I am incredibly appreciative to Wing for taking time out of his crazy, busy life and schedule to do just that. More importantly, I am looking forward to our growing friendship in making a positive difference for leaders. I love their trademark saying, "Drop in. Have Fun. Eat Well.™" It honestly is how my hubby and I choose to live our lives every day! #Wahoos #Dropin #HaveFun #EatWell #FoodFriendsandFamily #OurKindaPeople #SameSame #GotWing(s) #WeDo #LuckyPirates

To all of the many amazing leaders who are truly player-coaches: Dean Erickson (Deano), Suzanne Davis (SuzyD), Paul Golden, Cil Smith, Jorge Reyes, Ramon Bonilla, Brady Hogan and my OC and Chi-town leaders. I can't possibly name you all . . . the list would go on and on. These are just a few from so many exceptional people-leaders. A common quality they all share is their undeniable passion for people science, as well as for the business—plus, they are an absolute blast to have as #PeoplePartners! What really stands out for me, however, is how much these leaders care about people—and how much their people will do for them. #People1st #EpicCoaches #TheyDontCareHowMuchUKnow #UntilTheyKnowHowMuchUCare

#DreamTeams, you know who you are, I offer you my heartfelt gratitude for an exceptional ride! I am so lucky to have had you on my teams and in my life—what an epic journey indeed! Cheers to all of you! #UnderPressure #Village #Park #Green #GoWest #PushPull #MyKinfolk

Thank you to all of the leaders and mentors who have invested in and shaped me over the years. A few of you, I owe and offer my heartfelt apologies and gratitude for tolerating me during my more ass, less badass periods. Thank you to Greg Mutz, John Allen, Peggy Butterworth, Frank Romano, Mark Supena, Carla Kennedy, Lela Cirjakociv, Max Gardner, Kevin Baldridge, Troya Montgomery, Scott Reinert, Lori Torres, Kim Swetnam, and a special thank you to My Badass5thGradeTeacher, Jerry Linkhart. To Patti Cain-Stanley and massive thanks and appreciation to Mark Reines. I could never have grown so much without everyone's incredible guidance and support. Thank you all for making a positive difference in my life. #MyTeachers #Footprints #Starfish #Wings #Helmet #12Lessons

A very special thanks to all of these truly Badass Co-Leaders who have positively impacted my life and supported me through my sprouting entrepreneurial "growing my wings" stage. Thank you Rodrigo Carranza and J.T. Metzger for taking a chance and choosing the #DarkHorse! Massive Hugs of gratitude to Dr. Blair McConnell and Dr. Mark Eisenhart for your passionate support and #CuriousHunger. To my friend Deb VanCleve for being a #BadassMentor during my #SayYes then figure out how periods #RanchLife. To Joyce Schaefer who has always been so generous with her lessons, tools, friendship and stories, #LessonandVino. To Richard Branson who has no idea how much he has inspired me! #BeLikeBranson

To my #Chi-TownBFFs a.k.a. #MichelleX2—Michelle Stromberg Ohlhaber, Michelle Andres Fitz-Henry, and my local #BFF Marlene Bentson, #BadassCowgirl Paula Wittler, #TNT Tery Tanner and #BadassCowboy Tracy Vigil—I love and adore you guys. We need more time for FoodVinoHorsesCigarsand#2!

Thank you to Bryan H. Carroll and the makers and cast of the Badass movie *Why We Ride!* As a family, this movie really touched us, and we felt like it was our story too! Riding, camping and family go together and are passions for us. Check it out! *Why We Ride,* Amazon Prime Video, DVD, directed by Bryan H. Carroll, USA, 2013. #MakingMemories #DirtPlay #LivetoRide #WeAreGroupies4 #WhyWeRide

Thank you to my *From Bad to Badass Leader* Book Launch Team, my author and BestSeller in a Weekend coach, Alicia Dunams, Badass Graphic Designer—Bradlee Keith Steliff; my Boss Girl Genius attorney Raye Mitchell, and proud to call a friend and website guru extraordinaire, Brandy Thaler-Evans, a.k.a. #MagicFairy!

My heartfelt and respectful gratitude to those who #LivetoFeed. I'm humbled. For almost seven years I have had the incredible privilege of serving those who feed our country, our communities and our family. #ThankYouFarmers #PleaseThankaFarmer

Sincere thank you to all of those who serve and protect our country, our streets, our families and our freedom. Be safe and THANK YOU for your service, commitment and your sacrifices. #LivetoServe #FirePoliceMilitaryService #FirstResponders #SomeGaveAll #LetFreedomRing #FuckCancer

A special thanks to Tony Robbins and Cloe' Madanes for the incredible opportunity to become a certified Strategic Interventionist. It truly has helped bring the badass possibilities for my business to life, enabling me to make a positive impact for leaders, teams and organizations. #BadassGuru #ChangingLives

Thank you to my Wiley Authorized Partner Family, and for the many incredible authors and Badass Leaders who've paved the way and continue to develop and inspire me daily. Patrick Lencioni, Simon Sinek, Chi-town gal Oprah Winfrey, Maria Schriever, Gary C. Kelly, and Love-em Up Al Mulally. Thank you for setting the bar for me to follow. I will forever be a student, curious and hungry to learn more about how I can inspire other leaders to bring out the best in their people. #MakingImpossible #Possible #BeingLikeMaxFactor

Thank you to my amazing and talented clients, whose faith and commitment to MDR Coaching & Consulting, Inc., has enabled me to scale our impact, our collective success, and introduce this unconventional Badass Leader brand! #NotYourMothersLeadershipBrand #ThisBrands4U

I will end with a toast of #CasamigosReposado—cheers to all of you on your Badass Leader ride. #WorkHard #PlayHarder #NotTheEnd #TheBeginning #LoveSomebodyLikeU

STAY CONNECTED

I invite you to #JointheClub where you can share your #BadassStories, struggles and lessons learned with other #BadassLeaders. Connect with us and Join the Club at https://badassleader.com/ and while you're there, be sure to check out the toolboxes and events on our website. Our Facebook Badass Leader Members Club is a cool place to tap into other leaders and mentors to build your tribe—and recommend great tequilas. Most importantly let's stay connected and keep this party going! #JointheClub #ExpandyourTribe #Callme #HoveringOverThePhoneLikeTeenagers

LET'S GET PERSONAL

When I'm not writing or supporting leaders, I love to play hard and have fun dry camping in the desert, under the stars with my family and friends. I absolutely love 4-wheeling, riding dirt bikes, quads and horses, and going on rides or drives with my love. I live for epic date nights with my #BadassHubby. Our happy place is really anywhere together, but we much prefer hanging out back, fireside, with great food, vino, and tequila, surrounded by friends and family! #DTLove #Priorities #HappyLife #AttitudeofGratitude #MoreTimefor#2 #LivetoLove #Ciao4Now

WANNA HIRE US OR PARTNER?

Give us a RING or shoot us an EMAIL at info@badassleader.com.

We'll get back to you in 2 shakes of a lamb's tail! #2Shakes

#Callus

1-800-213-0612

Follow Us at:

 @BadassLeader12

 https://www.linkedin.com/in/michelle-d-reines

 badassleader12

 BadassLeader12@MichelleReines

Made in the USA
San Bernardino,
CA